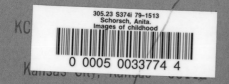

Images of Childhood

Images of Childhood
AN ILLUSTRATED SOCIAL HISTORY

ANITA SCHORSCH
FOREWORD BY ROBERT COLES

A Main Street Press Book
Published by Mayflower Books, Inc., U.S.A.
New York

Library of Congress Catalog Card Number 78-20363

ISBN 8317-4875-3

Published by Mayflower Books, Inc., U.S.A.

575 Lexington Avenue, New York City 10022

Produced by The Main Street Press, Inc.

42 Main Street, Clinton, New Jersey 08809

Designed by Al Cetta

Printed in the United States of America

To my husband and children

Contents

Foreword

We are glutted with books about what to do about our children; they are an obsession of many secular Americans who have given up on just about everything and everyone, except themselves and their extensions, a child or two or three (usually) whom mothers and fathers try to "rear" with an earnestness and competence that is all too often certified by others—our "experts" on childhood. What we want, so often, is advice, techniques, lists of oughts and noughts—and not least, sanction. Commonly without religious faith, and not so sure of our nationalism, either, we cling to the recommendations of doctors or psychologists with respect to the next generation: the only credible future in a world that sometimes seems on the verge of extinction.

So much of what we read and hear is glib or clever, but also banal, and certainly, a-historical; that is, suggestions rendered with self-important authority by individuals who have no sense of what childhood itself has or has not meant over the decades, the centuries. As fad gives way to fad, one might expect a spell of boredom, then skepticism to fall in: why worry so very hard about every move a child makes? Why not try to do the best one can, taking in what reasonable help there is, but ultimately remembering that there are no complete answers—and often only mysteries and ambiguities that give way to new mysteries, new ambiguities? When Anna Freud after a half decade of psychoanalytic work with children can recite what she calls "a long series of trials and errors" (*Normality and Pathology in Childhood*, 1965) one might think the rest of us would be ready for a longer view of what child-rearing has been about— indeed, what the very words "child" and "childhood" have meant over the centuries, within the context of Western history, never mind the history of other peoples, say, in Africa or Asia.

This book provides such a view—a much needed ground of distance for us to stand on. The author wants us to see children as others have seen them. She wants us to understand other times—beliefs and aspirations at variance with ours. She wants to tell us about that, but also, through excellent illustrations, she enables us to use our eyes. She wants us to know about "centuries of childhood", an apt phrase used by Philippe Aries to remind us that nothing, not even the essentials of life itself—a man, a woman, a child—escapes history and culture. It matters not only where we are born,

9

and to whom, but when—a commonplace that may easily be overlooked in a culture somewhat removed from its own past, and all too preoccupied with its own distinctive habits.

It would be something of a step for all of us in this time of our nation's life—and in this, the International Year of the Child—if Anita Schorsch's remarkable book were to obtain the wide audience it deserves. She is a strong, clear-headed writer. She is a social historian, able to give us a sense of how it has gone for children, for their parents, too, over the generations. She is a first-rate art historian; she understands how artists, well known and not known at all, have come to terms with children—with the imperatives of a given era. She has gathered a compelling series of illustrations, wedded them to a vigorous, knowing text, and so doing, made us a most valuable gift.

One can only hope that the "message" comes across loud and clear to a nation's people who badly need exposure to what comes across on the following pages: a reminder of how others felt, and struggled, and faltered and managed, somehow, to survive—or alas, not to last very long at all. A reminder that children have always been, and still are, a mirror to us—ourselves writ small, so to speak. When we have been at the very edge of survival, they are us, no more or less: mere life, lucky to have a next breath. When we have been on top of everything, but not sure where we are going or why, they are us, too: pampered and coddled and fretted over and held up to high heaven—a rock for the supposedly mighty to hold, and thereby forget those intimations of mortality that it is our peculiar fate to have as human beings. And all sorts of shades in between—children as young and burdened workers, or shrewd cynics, or indulged brats. Children as expressions of a dream, a determination, a rise, a decline. Children as instruments of parental intentions, or as labor, pure if not so simple. Children as God's Will, and children as man's stubborn, unyielding pride.

In a good moment, culturally, this book would be welcome news—something for all of us to read, look at, learn and learn from. I doubt it will come near replacing the various guides to "parenting" which, taking advantage of our nervous gullibility, continue to appeal for our money and time. But it is too bad one has to say that; and one can hope and pray for a turnaround, starting with the publication of *Images of Childhood*, a wonderful gift of social history, art history—the result of a high order of intelligence put to work writing words and selecting, arranging pictures.

Robert Coles
Cambridge, Massachusetts

Introduction

What is a child save a lower animal in
the form of man?
                    Luis De Granada (c. 1555)

Most modern readers will be startled to learn that the best thinkers of the 16th century, and of the preceding centuries as well, agreed that the child is nothing more than a lower animal—"the infant mewling and puking in the nurse's arms," as Shakespeare put it baldly, but succinctly. For so long have we respected the sweetness, innocence, and intelligence of the child, accepting the early years as the most important and the most formative in the life of a human being, that we find it almost impossible to believe that our ancestors once thought otherwise. Is it possible that the beautiful child we instinctively want to cuddle and to hold was called by Ralph Waldo Emerson only a century ago "a curly, dimpled lunatic"? Or that the otherwise civilized and droll English essayist Charles Lamb could have written the following in a personal letter to a friend:

> We have had a sick child, who, sleeping or not sleeping, next to me, with a pasteboard partition between, killed my sleep. The little bastard is gone.

The little bastard is gone. Was the life of the child in any century ever so expendable as to warrant that unfeeling epitaph?

Images of Childhood is an informal history of what it was like to be a child in the centuries before our own. It is a book of surprises, a compilation of historic information—textual and visual—so little known to modern parents that it should go a long

11

way, Ecclesiastes to the contrary, in illustrating that there is indeed plenty that is new under the sun.

Most of us would like to believe that family life has always revolved about the child; that mother, father, and baby have constituted a domestic trinity as old as Western civilization itself; and that the nursery was always the most beloved and sanctified room in the family house. The reality is that until fairly modern times most children were either abandoned by their mothers or farmed out to other women shortly after birth and that, in fact, both the family and the family house as we know them today did not even exist until well into the 17th century.

This book in no way pretends to completeness (a definitive history of childhood has yet to be written, and, if it were, it would run to many, many volumes). It does, however, touch upon some of the more provocative changes in the life of the child from the Middle Ages through the 19th century. If its first aim is to bring forward some fascinating information about the nature and nurture of children, known perhaps to scholars, but generally unfamiliar to the "common reader," its second aim is to explain

2. *Madonna and Child,* Cornelis van Cleve, Flemish, 16th century.

how the changing attitudes towards children over centuries of time have been reflected in the visual arts. In this sense, *Images of Childhood* can perhaps be best described as an adventure in seeing. The book begins in the Middle Ages and ends in the late Victorian era—when photographic images were rapidly replacing those of the pen and brush and when the young Freud was beginning the psychiatric "ministry" that would eventually replace that of the church in shaping and explaining the contours of childhood.

The opening chapter of Genesis has provided us with perhaps the best reason for having children and for disciplining them—"Be fruitful and multiply and fill the earth and subdue it." So let us, then, like Genesis, begin at the beginning.

Although they were hardly "real," the first children of Western civilization to be pictured on vases, tombs, and walls were the Greek putti, the little fat, playful babies who brought with them all the evil and the good spirits of the "other world." They represented love—erotic and spiritual—and they represented death, the fleeing of time and the soul returning. Supposedly, putti or genii were assigned to each newborn baby to

3. *The Christ Child and St. John with a Lamb,* Bernardino Luini, Italian, 16th century. John and Jesus, far from being "real" children, are depicted as cherubs without wings — that is, as putti. One aspect of authentic childhood, however, is present. Both figures grab and pull the fleece of the lamb as only curious human children would. The lamb suggests the innocence and submissiveness of Jesus.

guide and protect him throughout his life and were spirits that remained on earth after human death to be placated and comforted until they were again assigned to new babies. Pictured in medieval manuscripts, and painted decoratively and symbolically on church walls and ceilings, in homes on painted wall cloths, and worked into needlework and tapestry hangings, putti were beautiful and appealing. Their wingedness and their nakedness were meant to symbolize the power and the innocence of divine sovereignty.

Childlike images began, then, as reflections of the supernatural world, semimythical figures of picture magic. Like seeds of the devil mixed with seeds of the divine, putti were willful and rebellious in character, or guileless and pure. Like human children, but oddly without sex more often than not, they were made to appear playful, kissable, and hugable at one instant and like beasts nursing and tearing at the breasts of the classical Terra in another. They were symbolic children, of course, but their childish traits mirrored the observations of centuries of parents.

In the Middle Ages children were generally ignored until they were no longer children—that is, until they exhibited the attitudes of adults. Age through the 16th century, therefore, was more often measured by attitude than by chronology. In their first days, babies—both poor and rich—were separated from their mothers and were sent out to wet nurses. As children of eight or nine years they were again sent out—this time to the streets, where, accompanied by a slightly older child, but otherwise quite alone, they found work, lodging, and—if lucky or so inclined—a free school that would take them in. Children of the well-to-do followed this same pattern of being "put out" at birth and of once again leaving home in early childhood for apprenticeship or service, although they were more likely to have been placed with a family of their own choosing and of their own social class.

Although there are always exceptions to the rule, medieval communities dealt with their children as they dealt with their animals—and in the same practical and unsentimental way. Both shared the floor, the worms, the dirt, and every manner of disease that being a dog or a child in this period invited and implied. In perhaps one way alone children were uniquely different from the animals with whom they wallowed: Children were treated as if they were expendable. And expendable they were indeed, because in their first few years they died in droves. Perhaps to offset the horrors of an incredible rate of infant mortality, parents consciously limited affection and attachment to their children by putting them out in infancy and again at seven or eight years. Ironically, these physical and psychological separations sometimes contributed to the high infant death rate. And since women—breeders of babies, and little more—were almost as dispensable as children, there could always be more babies from where the dead ones had come. The lack of medieval family portraits, then, the absence of any sort of images of the earthly, living, breathing child, can be understood within this grim context: Children were replaceable because they had to be, and pictures of them would have been unwanted reminders of too many painful memories.

In contrast to the ugly realities of medieval infancy stand the many sacred births and scriptural childhood scenes depicted in medieval art, beginning with the Nativity, that are of almost unearthly beauty. People were fascinated, for example, with the birth of the girl Mary and mystified by God's choice of holy mother. Pictures of her in the borning room, being bathed and attended by the midwife and the wet nurse, appeared frequently in psalters and books of hours. The infancy of Moses, Jesus, and John, subjects of early woodcuts, also reflect conditions of medieval babyhood, ideal and real. Moses, abandoned, floats down the river in his swaddling clothes and is saved miraculously by God's divine instrument, the Pharaoh's daughter. He is nurtured by a Hebrew wet nurse who, *mirabile dictu*, turns out to be his own mother. Moses, unlike the medieval child turned out at infancy, is protected by his heavenly father and nur-

4. *Birth of the Virgin*, Israhel van Meckenem, German, 15th century. In one artistic moment we are shown events prior to, during, and after the birth of Mary— from the conception (*upper right*) to the lying in (*upper left*) to the delivery by midwives (*center right*) to the loving manner in which the infant is bathed. Note the cradle (with ties for securing the child) that will be seen in many of the illustrations following.

tured by the mother of his own blood. The depiction of Moses's early days, therefore, mirrors the struggle implicit in medieval infancy and in medieval mothering.

Although every aspect of life of Jesus—from Nativity to Ascension—has been illustrated through the centuries, illustrations of Jesus's infancy have always been the most popular. Although Jesus is described in Luke 2:12 as "a babe wrapped in swaddling clothes," he is more often shown unwrapped, free, and unrestrained—or in the manner of what one medieval encyclopedist would have called "a playful little boy." Jesus is portrayed as an affectionate infant who loves his mother, his arms unencumbered and free to caress and touch her as she holds him. Together, mother and child glorify the maternal image. Significantly, this reciprocal love between infant and mother was lost in the 17th century as a consequence of a major historical phenomenon: the polarization and isolation of the ages, sexes, and classes. Because of radical changes in society that will be explored in the chapters that follow, the easy union of spirituality and humanity, of man and God, of child and adult, of reason and sensuality—all symbolized by the love of Jesus and Mary—were difficult to sustain until the sacred and medieval position of mother and child was revived in 19th-century spirituality and was in turn reinterpreted by the generation of Freud.

If depictions of divine infants were common in the Middle Ages, realistic portrayals of ordinary children first appeared in the 15th century on the cornerstones of Italian

5. *The Finding of Moses*, woodcut from the *Schatzbehalter* by Stefan Fridolin, German, 1491. After the swaddled infant Moses is saved from the Egyptian execution of the first born (*upper right*), the baby is discovered in the bulrushes by the handmaidens of Pharaoh's daughter while his natural mother looks on overjoyed (*center left*). Although a literal rendering of the biblical story, the scene reflects the medieval practice of putting children out.

altarpieces. Interestingly, these reliefs do not depict the children alone as a fitting subject of the artist's attention, but as diminutive members of a family group. In these sculpture groups to patron saints, the children are generally seen kneeling in order of their size. Later in the same period, images of children also appeared on the tombs of deceased parents and teachers. By the 16th century, mothers and children of royal families were painted together, but not yet in an affectionate family manner. Appearing somewhat stiff and formal to modern eyes, these paintings are instead statements of aristocratic family background and wealth. Although the father is often absent from these portraits, his presence is nonetheless immediate and paramount in the sitters' rich trappings and ancestral lineage.

One of the most significant events in the history of the child and, of course, in the reflection of the child in art occurred in the 17th century when the structure of the modern family was first more or less set. Although the development of the family will be discussed in some detail in the chapters that follow, the 17th-century family—in brief—became a group united in one house, a group that was less loyal to ancestors and kin than to its immediate living-in members—wives, children, resident servants, indentured apprentices, and borders. The modern family was, in effect, a group bound by privacy, affection, and increasing personal freedom.

As the lords of manorial communities divested themselves of large tracts of land, and as smaller communities began to form, the home began to be associated more with familial and less with manorial loyalties. When the conditions of family life became easier for the "middling sort" of people, especially for yeomen and merchants, and they had time to turn inward to enjoy their conjugal families and, in particular, their children, domestic activities were for the first time profusely recorded in diaries and depicted in paintings. The Dutch were perhaps the first to celebrate the common non-aristocratic family in paintings set in such common settings as the interior of the house. They were the first, as well, to hang this art in the home, rather than in the church where, of course, depictions of the holy infant would have been found. This social phenomenon, beginning in 16th-century Dutch families and culminating in English and American Victorian families in the 19th century, was essentially the excitement of the developing family household and its accumulated material things. And, of course, the result was an art that recorded those material things, an art that not only appreciated children but depicted them enjoying material objects within and without the house. It is hardly an exaggeration to say that the thin line that separates the ancient regime from the modern world was breached when artists began to record with pen or paint the memories and human attachments that suddenly seemed more permanent than in the past and therefore worth preserving.

When the 17th-century social, economic, political, and religious reformations tore asunder the established leadership of the Middle Ages, the father of each household had laid upon him new responsibilities once assumed by the lord of the manor and the priest. As we shall see in forthcoming chapters of this book, the Protestant pater-familias was allowed and encouraged to pray and to preach as well as to protect the family. In his new role, he became the embodiment of power and of benevolence. He made his children subjects as well as objects of instruction and labor. With the new spiritual reforms that encouraged people to read, and the technological advances in printing and in the making of paper that took the Bible out of the church and placed it in the home, parents were enabled to put the word of God into the hands and hearts of children. Nurtured on the promise of spiritual and material rewards for goodness, and weaned on domestic sermons about the horrible consequences of sin and trans-gression, the child became not only a servant of God, but of his natural father as well—a reflection, in short, of his own and his father's sin and salvation.

Seventeenth-century man and his child had therefore grown away from the com-munal life of the Middle Ages—from the days when living did not revolve around the individual; when man was not the measure of all things; when rights, privileges, free-dom, and happiness for individuals had not been primary goals. The Middle Ages had

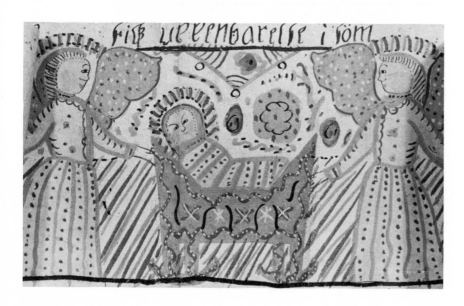

6. *Holy Child and Angels*, artist unknown, Swedish, 19th century. Unlike the infant Jesus portrayed in fig. 2, a child free to touch and love his mother, this northern Protestant folk art painting represents the Christ child as both swaddled and strapped in his cradle.

been a period of time in which either the community survived or no one survived; when the lord, the laborer, and the church depended on harmony between classes and between ages. But by the 17th century, each man, woman, and child was no longer responsible for the well-being of his neighbor, or for his neighbor's bad behavior or his neighbor's child. In the 17th century, man—for good or for ill—exchanged communal responsibility for privacy and individual freedom. As a result, the value of the individual rose and the corresponding interest in childhood as an isolated event, a particular age, and a worthy study was born.

Images of Childhood, by using the impact of these 17th-century societal changes as its focal point, and by looking backward to the communal experience of the Middle Ages and forward to the romanticism of the late 18th and early 19th centuries and the Victorianism of the later 19th, chronicles the development of the child—in history and in its reflection in art—through the dawn of the 20th century. Its pages reveal how the 17th century was marked by a new care and concern for childhood that could be called

7. *The First Born*, Samuel Dirksz van Hoogstraten, Dutch, 17th century. The Dutch were among the first to celebrate the common non-aristocratic family in painting. Here, within the setting of the house, a mother, attended by another woman, looks on her child with loving attention. The infant is neither swaddled nor strapped in its cradle.

at once both a cleansing and a controlling of the child; how the training, feeding, clothing, educating, and apprenticing of the young were aimed at achieving these goals; and how children were indoctrinated in the belief that industriousness and piety were the only roads to happiness. It further demonstrates how, in the 18th century, the child was granted a reprieve with time off for good behavior from the grim grayness of the Age of Faith after Rousseau and other modern writers found his natural beauty worth enjoying—and leaving alone. And through topics as diverse as the toys that some Victorian children were permitted to play with while others toiled in the cotton mills, it shows how the 19th century eventually returned the child to the moral thrall of the 17th:

> All children have wicked hearts when they are born; and that makes them so wicked when they grow up into life. Even little infants, that appear so innocent and pretty, are God's little enemies at heart.

8. *Portrait of an Elderly Gentleman with His Granddaughter,* attributed to Francisco Dei Rossi, Italian, 16th century. The family patriarch, loving but protective of his small granddaughter, evinces in his very pose the mixture of parental concern for children and their control by adults that have characterized the relationship between children and their fathers since at least the 17th century.

These words—written not by the pilgrim fathers of the 17th century, but by Samuel Spring, a best-selling children's writer in the "enlightened" 19th century—are in their own way an infinitely darker statement of the nature of children than those uttered more than two centuries earlier by John Earle, Bishop of Salisbury:

> A child is a man in a small letter, yet the best copy of Adam before he tasted of Eve or the apple.

Here, two centuries before we would most expect to find it, is the child defined as the very image of innocence: an Adam in miniature before the Fall—in short, "a man in a small letter."

How the child was seen through the centuries as both the incarnation of sin and as the epitome of innocence, and how these conflicting attitudes are reflected in art, form the core of this book. *Images of Childhood* records the changing fortunes of that most engaging and perplexing of creations—the child—called by philosophers and churchmen and teachers an invention of the devil and of angels, but perhaps best described by the poet Christopher Morley as "the greatest poem ever known."

9. *Francis O. Watts with Bird*, John Brewster, Jr., American, 1805.

1.

The Nature and
Nurture of Children

Of all the months the first behold,
January two-faced and cold.
Because its eyes two ways are cast,
To face the future and the past.
Thus the child six summers old
Is not worth much when all is told.
16th-century rhyme

Childhood in the 16th century was the least important of the twelve stages then believed to make up the evolution of man. Like the icy month of January to a farmer
waiting to plant seed, children were considered a worthless season "without wit,
strength, or cunning." They could accomplish nothing profitable. Childhood was of
little consequence and even less social value until the 17th century, and was therefore
rarely measured unless a father counted the number of teeth in his child's mouth or, as
a Quaker schoolmaster suggested, one noticed when a child could distinguish his right
hand from his left.

Infant, baby, child, and *youth* were interchangeable words. A lack of public concern for the very question of age left the parish priests with the job of keeping ages
registered, and as clerks they were not very systematic. But it did not matter, because
children went to school and to work when the parents were simply ready for them to
leave home—in general, when they needed the room and the privacy from a child
growing rebellious and sexually alert.

Of the many ages of mankind, the medieval mind recognized at least four ages of
childhood, all attested to in the iconography of contemporary woodcuts—the naked
age, the swaddled age, the robed age, and the hobby-horse age, or, as some woodcuts
depict them, the cradle age, the walker age, the hobby-horse age, and the school age.
Only in sexual maturity, or in what was then called "the condition and predicament of

23

being able to beget children," was there a definite signal that all the ages of childhood were over. The recognition of childhood as occurring after infancy at a particular age, such as three, and reflecting a particular attitude, such as innocence, is a modern concept, one completely undefined in the distant past. The thought of children as being different from adults simply did not exist, in fact, until the 17th century, when children were finally isolated from the family and community in which they were once integral members in all aspects of daily life, including play, education, work, and familial intimacy.

Not age, but the moment of birth—the month, the day, and the hour—gave the fateful twist to the life of the medieval child, setting each child in its astrological orbit and determining the character, complexion, and temperament of each. The discovery of new stars in 1618 reinforced the theory of planetary influence on the innate character of children just as it contributed to the cyclical theory of history, the decline and fall of nations, and the expectation of the end of the world. Astrological and biological determinism, needless to say, made child-rearing practices seem irrelevant. Like the features on children's faces, time was seen to enlarge the character but not to change it.

Assigning children numerical age, then, was first associated with astrology. Through the stars, children were connected to the ancient and divine system of num-

bers that placed all vegetable and animal growth into their own ratios of space and time. Everything in the medieval world—art, architecture, religion, and life itself—depended upon a knowledge of numbers and of ratios. All beauty in living, according to St. Augustine, was a matter of right proportions and the harmony of numbers. Understanding one's number—that is, his place in the divine scheme of things—made life comfortable, secure, orderly, and therefore beautiful.

By the end of the 15th century the numbers *seven* and *fourteen* were already associated with childhood. Seven was a lesser number separating the infant-child from the reasonable child and the toy-playing child from the reading child and the servant, ending the period of "effeminacy" and beginning the rite of passage for boys—a time when apprenticeship contracts were first to be drawn up. It was a time, in later centuries, of clothing change—generally from dresses to breeches—and coincided with the religious crises which parents stirred in the child of seven.

Fourteen meant the end of schooling in the medieval three R's—reading, writing, and religion—the end of indulgent and irresponsible behavior, the end of forgiveable sin as well as of divine innocence, and even the end, for many, of all other aspects of education and apprenticeship. After the Reformation, the age of fourteen was a time of blossoming religious conversions in Calvinistic or evangelical families—and a time of

10. *Bartholomew Fair in 1721.* Bartholomew Fair, which had had its origins in the Middle Ages, was together with other fairs and places of public assembly eschewed by the pious as "sinks of sin." This view of the fair in the 18th century demonstrates how the spirit of the Middle Ages was annually revived in a communal display of entertainment for all ages alike, including the smallest of children.

11. *The Ages of Man*, woodcut from *Le Proprietaire des Choses* by Bartholomaeus Anglicus, French, 1482. Of the seven ages of man understood by the medieval mind, four encompassed childhood: the infant (tied in its cradle); the walking child (with an early walker); the playing child (with hobby-horse); and the young scholar (wearing the long robe of the student).

frequent suicides. It was a time of marriage for many girls, and in the 20th century, of course, was stretched into a prolonged period of childhood called adolescence.

Sex influenced a child's place on the hierarchical ladder. The birth of a boy child was favored in the home and in the courts. Inheritance laws for the middle and upper classes provided for lineal passage of land and property through legitimate sons, bastards, and half siblings, until church and state reclassified the legal status of marriage contracts to include only legitimate sons. The eldest son always received the estate of property. Because of the high mortality rate of children in the past, the eldest son was not always the first son, and there were times when younger boys had the opportunities accorded by law to the first born. Younger sons and girls generally received no land and had to consider whatever education fitted them best for the realities of the workaday world. Given the rigidity of the rule of primogeniture, material equality was therefore enjoyed only by medieval children when they were from families of the poor or the propertyless. But, of course, nothing divided equally still yields nothing.

Male children, naturally, inherited more than material goods alone. They were the proud possessors of what was conceived to be a rational nature suited only to the male of the species, a gift of reason that was to deepen as they grew. Boys were therefore expected to be leaders in the family and in the nation, and because of this consequence of possessing reason, they received a longer and more complete education. But it was also the boys who caused violence in the community, the boys who needed this violent aspect of their natures diluted by a mother and, later, a wife. Boys ten to twelve joined in the frenetic violence of the crowds during May Day festivals and psalm-singing parades. Sixteenth-century Protestant and Catholic children often marched in prayer, aggresively shouting and demonstrating for God, upsetting the other members of their communities with their religious rioting.

By no stretch of the imagination could a girl's number in the hierarchical system be ascendant. Considered of little "value," a girl child was less likely to survive infancy than was a male, and, if she did, she was even less likely to be educated. Girls, therefore, were subsumed by brothers, fathers, husbands, and sons and remained "inferior" from the cradle to the grave. Ancient records preserve one husband's instructions to his wife, explaining that if their child turned out to be a boy it should live, and, if a girl, it should die. Similarly, in the 18th century, sex frequently influenced the incidence of abandoned children and even affected the chances of adoption. One woman, waiting for the birth of a child who was to be cast out so that she could adopt it, wrote: "If it is a boy, I claim it. If it is a girl, I will be content to stay for the next."

Henry VIII was no happier to find that his newborn was the girl child Elizabeth. He refused to attend her baptism, and, when a family portrait was ordered, the future queen was not included in the picture.

The essential nature of girls was perceived, like the mystery of numbers, to be intimately connected to the fate of the stars, the cycle of the seasons, and the physiology of the humors. Because of the fluids or juices of bile, blood, and phlegm which dominated the body in conjunction with the four seasons, girls inherited "changeable, deceptive, and tricky temperaments." Where boys were thought to be restless and disorderly because of an unchristian and coarse upbringing, girls were thought to be disorderly *by nature* and were, like Eve, the very embodiment of the original sin of disobedience. Sixteenth-century medical opinion agreed that girls were made of cold and wet humors, while boys were the concoction of hot and dry humors. A girl was subject to her womb. It dominated her body and her mind, causing her to have what was believed to be an insatiable sexual appetite and to be prone to the sickness of hysteria, a disease known only to women until Freud in the 19th century discovered it in men. The magical cure for her ailments was a firm religious training. Her submission to the head of the household, as John Calvin saw it, was good preparation for loving God, the ultimate "head of the household."

12. *Birth of the Princess Elizabeth* and *Delight of Henry at Having a Son and Heir,* illustrations by John Leech for *The Comic History of England* (London, 1864). The birth of a girl-child in the past was not exactly an occasion for joy. The fathers of girls were called "buttonhole-makers" and other epithets even more vile.

Girl children were a liability to medieval parents. Crude pet names were given to them as a reminder of their inferior status. They were called "split pals" or "pissers," as one French schoolbook called them, while boys remained "the masterpiece." Yet the peculiar belief that the milk of mothers who bore girls was best for feeding boy babies was not only oddly contradictory, but had the effect of threatening the lives of girl babies through the removal of their very nourishment. Since chastity and fructification were both holy vocations, a girl, if she lived, could look forward to marriage or to a nunnery. She made her choice according to the practical needs, not of herself, but of her family. Whether parents could keep a girl until she married (which was sometimes as young as twelve) and whether they could provide a dowry sufficiently generous to make men want to take her to wife were pertinent questions of the day. In medieval times as in the modern era, in Europe as in the New World, a little girl could look forward to less change in her life than could a little boy—less change in education, which remained religious and domestic; in marriage, which continued as a property contract and a religious affiliation; and in ideal goals, which, molded by law, placed her in service to her husband, and through him into the service of God and country.

Beyond artistic representations of the Nativity story itself, there is very little art or literature that reflects attitudes of affection towards children much before the 17th century. Setting the first and most tender example of affection in childhood, the baby Jesus

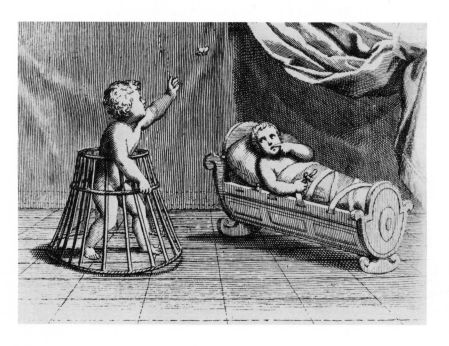

13. *Chasing Butterflies,* artist unknown, French, 17th century [reproduced from *Jeux* (Paris, 1900)]. This engraving clearly illustrates the constraints of the reforming mind of the 17th century. The infants are either tied tightly in the cradle or confined in a stationary basketwork pen to keep them off the floor. Curiously, there seem to have been no eyebrows raised at the phallic toys used as pacifiers or for teething.

—all powerful, yet helpless—played with his mother, touching her as she touched him, the liturgy lifting humanity and physical affection to higher levels than it was to go in the centuries that followed its inception.

The next singular, important, and very different document of physical "affection" is perhaps found in the 17th-century diary of the physician who attended the French baby and future king, Louis XIII. In a shocking record of sexual liberties, obscene language, and bold gesturing which belonged to the climate of the noble class and which filtered down to the more common classes as well, the little dauphin at three, four, and five years was manipulated, fondled, and made part of the sexual indecencies of adults. It was not uncommon for him to have spent time in the beds of his nursemaid, his governess, the servants, and the king himself, being played with, touched, and teased about his little genitals. But, because the nature of children under ten was interpreted as asexual, indifferent, and incorruptible, much like the offspring of animals, it was not considered untoward or immoral in contemporary adult eyes to subject children to the animal-like affection they might proffer a pet. A glance at the illustrations in medieval illuminated manuscripts reveals the commonness with which churchly figures were shown in what moderns might consider compromising or vulgar positions. But the events of daily life—including the suckling of the newborn, the circumcision of babies, the sexual play of young boys—were not hidden any more than were the sexually-tempted monk and the seductive woman. They were all aspects of life that had to be recognized and identified. (It was left to later, more fastidious generations to censure and censor in art a good portion of the events in human life.) Medieval illuminations provided an illiterate people with a way to know and recognize evil, and illustrations of the "good life" and of "good people" provided alternatives to profane pursuits. The traditional church, knowing the unmanageable elements in medieval life—the overwhelming cold, hunger, disease, and death—did not condone, but certainly did understand, the drunken, raucous society that was dulling its pain and soothing its heart in physical abandon.

Humanists and Protestant reformers of the 17th century, denigrating the pictorial use of holy figures in vulgar poses, nonetheless sensed that the unruly and passionate figures of man seemed to be fathered by the child. When the minister John Robinson spoke to American Pilgrims of children as "a blessing great, but dangerous," he was voicing a shared, instinctual fear of the evil affection in their nature. Samuel Davies, a New Light Presbyterian preaching in Virginia, called the child a "little wond'rous miniature of man . . . ," "an embryo angel," and "an infant fiend."

The new Calvinism envisioned every child as a bearer of natural sin. Resenting the indifference of medieval parental attitudes, Calvinists dealt with evil and sensuality in a repressive way. Rather than expose what they considered "black and ugly sin," they covered it up. Consequently, they must have been relieved to swaddle their babies, reducing a physically active infant to an immobile body and a docile mind. The heavy wrapping of swaddling clothes also prevented the free enjoyment of the pleasures of physical affection between parent and child. The Calvinistic wish to restrict the parent, we can conjecture, might have been as strong as the wish to restrict the child. Although functional and instructive, the walkers that supported babies before they were ready to stand were in their own way repressive, protecting them not only from falling, but from crawling on the floor and reminding their all too sin-conscious parents of the dirty state of animals and insects. Anxiety over the child's natural affinity to dirt was something new to the world of the family.

14. *Virgin and Child,* Studio of Cosimo Tura, Italian, 15th century. The bird on a string, symbolic of human mortality (and, hence, of the mortal aspect of Jesus), is free to fly only after death. Because of the horrendously high incidence of infant mortality in the past, the image of the child with a bird on a string or in a cage was immensely popular. (*See* figs. 9 and 15.)

From earlier times through the 18th century, children, like their parents, had been accustomed to the dirt of the house and of the street. Personal cleanliness could not very well be taken for granted at a time when latrines were virtually unknown in both the households of the rich and of the poor. In the language of the day, the public "did its business" on every street corner. The rare indoor privies that existed were in the homes of such exceptional people as the famous diarist Samuel Pepys. His connected to a tub in the cellar which was emptied by men who came in at night with buckets, loading their carts and dragging away the Pepys family's "night soil." Pepys commented that it turned his stomach when the men went through the house. Chamber pots, however, were more frequently used than privies. After formal dinners when men and women separated, they went their separate ways to use the potty chairs to accommodate their bodily needs. In wealthy homes parents were known to employ the services of a physician who would apply suppositories and purges to empty the child's bowels. Louis XIII

15. *Master John George Riedel,* artist unknown, American, c. 1850.

was trained in the carthartic way to use the chamber pot by the age of two. Though very little has been written on the subject of toilet training, it seems reasonable to assume that, since adults lived with the stench of urine in every stairwell and walked in streets littered with the reeking refuse of emptied chamber pots, children would be left dirty and untroubled by the anxiety psychoanalysts now call "anal fixation." But perhaps more to the point, in a world in which the sense of smell was assaulted on all sides by the stench of rotting human excrement, one can almost understand how the Calvinists came to associate the physical world—and especially that of the child—with sin and filth.

Physical restrictions accompanied the 17th-century restraints of the will. Baby girls went quickly into corsets and tight bodices in a continuation of the subjection of unpredictable female humors. An aggressive determination to weed out sin, "a stubbornness and stoutness of mind arising from natural pride, which must in the first place be broken and beaten down," grew as the Puritan body politic grew and spread through the middle class in 17th-century France, Puritan England, and Protestant America. Earlier, repressive disciplinary measures had been meted out by aristocrats of the 16th century and even by Henry IV, father of Louis XIII, who instructed tutors in the discipline of his young son:

> I wish and command you to whip him every time that he is obstinate or does something bad. . . . I know from experience that I myself benefitted, for at his age I was much whipped. That is why I want you to whip him and to make him understand why.

Such training or punishment, however, was not imposed until after Louis was six, and then it was administered in the spirit of training a young horse or hunting dog in order to improve performance rather than to develop in the child a moral state of being.

Still, the 17th-century attitude toward children was not entirely bleak. There exist many tender thoughts recorded in letters written by Anglicans, Quakers, and some Puritans, recognizing the delicacy of children as they flowered and the beauty and harmlessness of their ways. Children could indeed be loved when they were seen as harmless, or helpless—and especially when they were dead. They were like "tender plants growing in the Truth," as one Welsh Quaker wrote, or like 'Three flours, two scarcely blown, the last in the bud, Cropt by th' Almighties hand," as Anne Bradstreet wrote of her three grandchildren who had died. Sentimental comparisons of children to virtuous flowers and timid animals appeared occasionally and then more frequently in the literature as well as in the genre painting and engraving of the late 17th century.

The discovery of childhood evils was therefore balanced by the delight taken in childhood affections. On the one hand, children were beaten, and, on the other, they were treated like lovely harmless birds, holy little doves. Consequently, when portraits of children became numerous by the beginning of the 18th century, the sitters were frequently painted together with the divine lamb and with the martyred goldfinch of Jesus and John. The harmless bird and lamb were undoubtedly seen as the common attributes of the good spirit of children.

That by the end of the 17th century each child was finally perceived to have a soul of his own was soon reflected in the formal process of naming an infant. No longer did parents, mourning the past, pass down the same name used by one or more siblings who had died. Using the appendices of the Bible in which they found English meanings for scriptural words, Protestants enthusiastically created such unique names for their new babies as Tribulation Wholesome and Zeal-of-the-Land Busy. With greater confidence in the survival of infants and with a new literacy and love of Scripture, the large middle class named its babies in preparation for the new kingdom to come. It is easy to

16. *Sir Thomas Aston at the Deathbed of His Wife*, artist unknown, British, 1635. The high incidence of infant mortality was well matched by the deaths of both mother and child in childbirth. With the cradle of the deceased newborn draped in black and its mother laid out in white mourning reserved for the young or innocent, the surviving child in mourning clothes by the side of his grieving father is not spared the reality of death and holds a cross, a symbol of earthly mortality and the life to come.

forget that the Protestants of yesterday, from strict Puritan to enlightened Quaker, expected to live in an earthly community of saints where the supervision of evil would be unnecessary. The naming and raising of their chidren toward that end, in salvation and sainthood on earth, was a battle to defeat the devil in the child. To give the child a unique name was the new Protestant's way of saying, "I recognize you as an individual, and I am giving you your own soul." The 17th century had thus become a time when no one could any longer believe the early 16th-century saying, "Who sees a child sees nothing."

If the nature of children was once obscure, ill-defined, and unimportant to the community at large, then the nurture or care of children was equally unimportant. For the general reader and the scholar alike, the years before 1600—before modern religious,

17. *Little Girl with Flowers and Dog,* artist unknown, Dutch school, c. 1690. Dressed in the restraining stays of the 17th century, this child—painted to look older than her years—is obviously still an infant. Notice the teething ring in her hand and the phallic whistle that hangs at her side. The tight bodice of her costume was soon to be criticized for causing "Narrow Breasts, short and stinking Breath, and ill Lungs and Crookedness."

economic, and educational reform—seem like times of distant and superficial relations between parent and young child. Natural parents in the context of their social class had little time, and made little time, to become affectively attached to the young child. Consciously directed affection was given hesitantly or abusively, with little regard for what modern parents would call "the child's needs." The enormously high mortality rate of infants in all classes, which must have produced great feelings of loss and perhaps the disease of hysteria to which women were told they were prone, spawned a custom called "putting out" which artificially separated mother from child so that natural parental affection could not grow until the child appeared to have survived the first years. Suckling was generally the work of wet nurses from rural areas, women who had just borne their own children and either weaned them to pap or abandoned them. Despite their life-giving calling, they were often unable to provide proper nourishment for someone else's infant or even the proper environment. Although the country air was regarded as good for babies, the rural nurses themselves tended to be dirty, underfed, and overburdened with the demands of their own families and

18. *Woman Making Lace*, Nicolaes Maes, Dutch, 17th century. Although this small child appears restrained and bored, he is actually well tended by 17th-century standards. The highchair, which is closed across the front, has a small shelf below for a footstove to warm the infant. The stove was interchangeable with a pot to allow the child to relieve itself during its long confinement. The baby, like infants in any century, has thrown its belongings on the floor for mother to pick up.

husbands who usually did not excuse them from their sexual responsibilities. Wet nurses were known to replace one child with another following the death of a "put-out" child without informing the natural parents of the tragedy or the replacement.

Although it was difficult to convince women and their husbands of the value in mothers suckling their own babies, especially in the 16th and again in the 18th centuries, the medical profession and the ministry pleaded for the natural mother to nurse "with her own unborrowed milk," a felicitous, but ironic phrase taken from the tombstone of one virtuous mother. Books on the government of children, written by apothecaries, or pharmacists as they would be called today, addressed fathers and mothers to let the child suck at his own mother's breasts:

> But why, you'll say, take pains to address each Parent distinctly? The reason is obvious. A Man cannot be conversant in Life, and not see that many a sensible Woman, many a tender Mother, has her Heart yearning to suckle her Child and is prevented by the misplac'd Authority of a Husband.

Physicians had spread the word that mother's milk from the breast of the woman who bore the infant provided the most safe, most nutritious, and most spiritually sound food a newborn could receive. Yet, in spite of the forbidding belief that had sur-

19. *A Reprimand*, artist unknown, French, 19th century [reproduced from *Jeux* (Paris, 1900)]. Keeping children clean and dry was no less an unpleasant task in the past than now and one that in moments of exasperation, especially with older children, led to reprimands and the inculcation of that most powerful of weapons—shame.

vived from the Middle Ages—that blood to the breasts changed into milk, implying that babies could be contaminated by the poor blood of a wet nurse—women long continued to be hired to suckle "put-out" children, and advertisements for wet nurses continued to be found even in colonial American newspapers. It was not until almost the 19th century that the practice died out in England and in America.

The child in the 17th century received more care, more discipline, more supervision, and more privacy than did the young of earlier periods of history. When church splinter groups evolved into small Protestant sects, and when small towns and small conjugal family units replaced larger communal and traditional church loyalties, families found themselves increasingly responsible for their own order and for their own pleasures. The swing away from dedication to the communal group, and the community's eventual division into small family units, each individually autonomous, both benefitted and burdened the child. No longer a free agent in the streets or a pet and plaything of the rich and their servants, the child was rapidly disciplined to be clean inside and out, to be kept safe in mind and body, to remain innocent and separate from worldly things, to be educated in useful pursuits and in pure thoughts. It would not be long before the orphans in the street would become the object of a public cleanup, receiving instruction in religion and virtue so that, according to the moral beliefs of the day, they might not remain poor or be susceptible to evil and thereby spread it. Parents, convinced of the need for a greater parental involvement in the lives of each of their own children and for a stronger wall against the evils in everyone else's children, pushed adulthood, the time of independent activity, even further away than it had even been from the growth and development of a child.

Many documents devoted to the subject of the nature and nurture of children appeared in the 18th century, most of them, however, being essays dealing with such moral subjects as "grievances of youth," "pollution in both sexes," proposals on education, duties of children to parents and parents to children, and "youthful inconstancy." Throughout the century, variations on these themes were published—the advantages of a well-ordered family, nursing and management of children, duties of the female sex, duties of the male sex, the government of children, spiritual counsel for children, education for the young nobility and gentry, and mercy to the children of the poor. Parents and children were mutually indoctrinated by these guidebooks and their up-to-the-minute advice. The Protestant ministers and the philosophical writers of the moment were, after all, the Gesells and the Spocks of yesterday.

Since the nature of the child, like the nature of the family, was perceived until the close of the 19th century in an almost exclusively religious light, it makes sense for us to comprehend the nature of child rearing in the past as our ancestors would have understood it. If a child's parents were typical Calvinists, the child was assumed to have been born sinful, and parents worked diligently to break the will, subdue the evil, and provide scriptural foundations for the new life abuilding. If, however, his parents were Unitarians, Deists, or members of the gentility, the child was treated as an innocent, and the parents had no reason to disturb his natural goodness by training him unduly. If, like John Locke, they were Anglicans, or if they were Friends and the child was born likened to "a white paper inscribbled with the observations of the world," then parents could more comfortably and moderately teach him the manner of logic or of "holy conversation." The need for discipline, therefore, was relative and was more vital to certain family temperaments than to others. Yet, as a general rule, the 17th century was "the great age of the whip." Protestants were whipped for leaving the church; beggars were whipped for being idle; unmarried mothers were whipped for their sexual degeneracy; children were whipped equally for exercising their wills and for not learning their Latin. As popular belief would have it, the reason for beating a boy's bottom was simple indeed:

20. *Two Sisters, Ann and Sarah,* artist unknown, American, c. 1800. Enjoying the outdoors as Rousseau had recommended, these young girls wear the high-waisted, loose-fitting dresses advocated by such early 19th-century childhood experts as Dr. Christian Augustus Struve who believed that tight stays and petticoats were "savage and unnatural" and led to "ruptures."

In every person there is a Good Spirit and an Evil Spirit. The Good Spirit has its own dwelling place—which is the head. So has the Evil Spirit—and that is the place where you get the whipping.

Violence to children from parents and teachers was socially acceptable. When before the Reformation children had been treated as domestic animals, discipline and training were considered wastes of time. But in the reforming spirit of the 17th century, when the nature of childhood was recognized as "curable," the twin offices of discipline and training developed important statures of their own. All the conditions of childhood living, and especially of childhood sleeping, were painstakingly scrutinized. Children were no longer encouraged to sleep in the same bed or in the same room with the valet, the maid-servant, the tutor, or even their parents. Cohabitation, generally—though widespread in all classes of society, in schools and at home—took

21. *Woman and Child,* artist unknown, British or American, 19th century. Plump, wholesome, and healthy, protected within her mother's arms, this infant reflects the concern for children that developed in the decades following the publication of such influential works as William Blake's *Songs of Innocence.* Note her teething ring and rattle. By the early 19th century, mother had begun her ascendance to the family throne.

on a certain reformed decorum. In addition, schools, masters, and tutors put new restraints on children and on themselves. That children should not be left alone was a rule first discussed in the 15th century, but not put into actual practice until the 17th. The most elite public schools continued to enforce flogging, to teach not the social deference of earlier centuries, but control of the will in preparation for sainthood. The Calvinist point of view in 17th-century England would continue in 18th-century American evangelical families with the same conviction. As Esther Edwards Burr, daughter of Jonathan Edwards and wife of Aaron Burr, wrote to a friend in 1754:

> I had almost forgot to tell you that I have begun to govourn Sally. She has been whip'd once on *Old Adams* account, and she knows the difference between a Smile and a frown as well as I do.

It was no different for John Wesley, the founder of Methodism, growing up in a late 18th-century evangelical home with a mother who disciplined him from infancy "to fear the rod and to cry softly." More than once was he whipped for the sake of our mythic father, "Old Adam." Similar governing regulations were repeated in contemporary American writings that, like the pious literature of the 17th century, advised parents that "the rod, judiciously administered, would effect subordination in children." The words of Solomon, quoted in a Connecticut advice book, were labeled "Passive Obedience": "Correct thy son whilst there is hope and let not thy soul spare for his crying." Parents, according to one author, Cyrus Comstock, had only a short time in which to provide a "government" for children, a set of rules—in short, a cage. The most frequent metaphoric allusion to child-nurture, in fact, was a cage where children could be kept safe, restricted, and forced to learn. As M. Cadet, a French pedagogue, put it:

> As far as possible, all the apertures of the cage must be closed. . . . A few bars will be left open to allow the child to live and to enjoy good health; this is what is done with nightingales to make them sing and with parrots to teach them to talk.

Perhaps M. Cadet, whose teaching methods were likened by his contemporaries to a birdcage, knew that the child, like a bird, would flutter sensitively and naturally near the open bars hoping someday to be free—perhaps only in death.

Children under the reform of the 17th century were not in any way to be pampered. Puppet shows and circuses, once ubiquitous sources of childish pleasure, were no longer respectable amusements for them. Many of the songs which were commonly sung were labeled indecent. Servants were suddenly suspect because they supposedly filled children with a love of gambling and amusement, and grandparents, because they made children vain.

Clothing children, like raising them, has been a problem only since the 17th century. As one perplexed observer put it:

> On cloathing Children . . . the grand Controversy is what kind of Cloaths they should wear, and how they must be put on; how Boys should be cloathed, and how Girls; what Cloathing conduces to Health, and what impairs it; with many other Things much disputed, but still unsettled.

Then, of course, there was the question of the *style* in which to dress children, a perennial problem, though of comparatively recent origin.

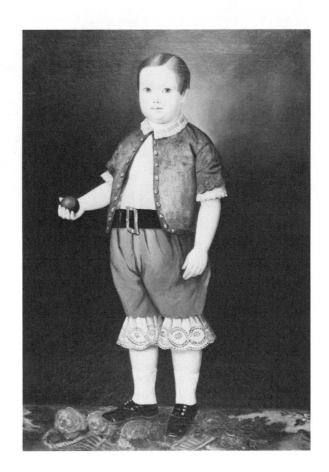

22. *Portrait of Master Dodson*, artist unknown, American, 19th century. Fat children may have been considered "jolly" by their mothers, but the late 18th-century child expert James Nelson warned them that "to be fat is one thing, and to be healthy another." "Fat," he admonished, "may be compared to ill-gotten Wealth; they both prey upon the Vitals." Master Dodson's unbuttoned suit, however, is not a result of obesity, but reflects contemporary fashion.

23. *Young Boy in Skeleton Suit* and 25. *Portrait of a Young Girl with Parasol,* both artists unknown, American, 19th century. Her costume places the little girl in the 1870s, but her insecurity, revealed as she clutches the ruffle of her skirt, identifies her as a child of any period.

24. *Frances and Charles Cowdry,* Henry Walton, American, c. 1838. Dr. Struve's *Domestic Education of Children* (1802) explained that if small children of both sexes were not dressed identically "the attention of children [would] be excited to the differences of the sexes, a circumstance which would deprive them, at an early age, of their innocence and happy ignorance."

Clothing is one more visible and material expression of child-rearing attitudes that reflect parental affection, consideration, anxiety, and even hostility. The late 18th century, for example, is characterized by a loosening of 17th-century restrictions, the clothes of the day suggesting both a lengthening of childhood and further separation of child and adult. Dr. Christian Augustus Struve, physician at Gorlitz and honorary member of the Royal Humane Society of London, addressed himself to the issue of clothing and good health in a book entitled *A Familiar View of the Domestic Education of Children* (1802). In it he proclaimed that:

> *The dress of children should be different from that of adults.* —It is disgusting to behold a child disfigured by dress, so as to resemble a monkey rather than a human creature . . . . A suitable dress for young people ought to shew, by the contrast it forms to that of adults, how far the latter have trespassed upon the laws of decorum, and how little attention is generally paid to health and convenience.

Dr. Struve was impressed by the ideals of child rearing described in Jean Jacques Rousseau's *Émile* (1762). Rousseau, of course, had observed that many defects found in a child's body and mind came from a desire to make adults of them before their time. Struve, consequently, wanted children to be free of physical and fashionable restraints. He insisted on throwing away "detestable swaddling clothes" and the "leading strings [which] have the appearance of a harness contrived for the taming of a wild animal." He encouraged mothers to use an approach in dress nearer to the standards of nature and "true task." Loose clothing, easier for the child to wear and easier for the mother to change when soiled, became the turn-of-the-century standards of good taste. Tying in and propping up, whether by bands, strings, stays, sashes, shoes, high breeches, or buckles, were, in Dr. Struve's opinion, savage and unnatural, leading in turn to a disease he called "ruptures."

By the beginning of the 19th century, the upper and middle classes extended the limits of childhood and successfully enclosed and defined it by adopting clothes especially designed for children. Girls were no longer rushed into looking like women, nor boys too quickly turned into men. But clothing, of course, had not always been a distinguishing feature of age or sex. Anglo-Saxon children until the end of the 10th century were brought up in the first years without any clothing at all. They appeared in the 11th in shirts and caps.

Prior to 1400 virtually every clothed European wore the same basic loose, cloak-like covers with slits on the sides and separate sleeves. By 1500 Western clothing had become what can be called "stylish" or "differentiating"—tighter and more binding for females, as well as for children of both sexes. A boy under six was dressed like a girl because his age made him subordinate, hence "effeminate." Girls, because of their sex, were considered subordinate at any age. But a boy would eventually reach the age of reason and grow out of his inferior status, being "breeched" in time to celebrate his rite of passage into the adult world—that is, the world of "reasoning" males. Girls, since biblical times a symbol of human weakness, remained forever in the clothing of the dependent class, never reaching a point in their maturation or in their dress to warrant a celebration.

Variations of robe, collar, and breeches were worn at different ages. The bib and tucker was a short robe and collar which belonged to the five-year-old. The frock was a long robe worn by ten-year-olds. Breeches were worn under their frocks by boys of six or seven. The skeleton suit, a shirt buttoned to the trousers and ruffled for upper-class boys, was the popular casual attire by the end of the 18th century, and may be seen to advantage in the rural look for boys so skillfully captured in the paintings of Reynolds,

26. *Beauty and Barbarism*, Lilly Martin Spencer, American, c. 1890. The title of this little-known Victorian painting is all-telling. The expression of the little "beauty" is identical with that of any child forced prematurely into the world of adult vanity.

Gainsborough, Copley, and Stuart. Such self-consciously rural attire enjoyed the look of innocence and health and reflected the popular enthusiasm among the better classes for Rousseau's ideas on the natural child.

Appearance signalled not only concern for sex, age, and class differentiation, but a concern for the healthy physical development of children. Fashion at the end of the 18th century reflected the medical opinions of the day. Buckled shoes became soft pumps at the same time that German and English doctors were recommending string laces in preference to buckles. People began to be concerned about tight shoes deforming children's feet and about poorly fitting shoes causing an unsafe gait. Healthful recommendations, such as wearing a kind of half-boot laced at the ankle for steadiness, were another indication that the cult of childhood that we know so well today had indeed arrived.

Hair at the end of the 18th century was still being cut at shoulder length, even though short hair had swiftly become the latest fashion. Large rims and low crowns on hats of straw or felt replaced the bonnet every child wore until he was five or six years old. Sometimes the cap—variously called a "black pudding," a "hot pie," or a "head cushion"—continued to be worn by lower-class boys. Hats carried a multitude of meaning, symbolic and otherwise. In the evangelical and genteel communities since the 1500s, the hat in hand had been a symbol of deference and subordination to parents and to God. To such members of the intellectual gentry as Rousseau, hats were indulgent and overprotective articles of clothing except under the most extreme conditions. Catherine Beecher informed her 19th-century American compatriots that bare heads, like bare feet exposed to fresh cold air, were good for children. A hat, Dr. Struve explained, generally promoted an accumulation of vapors and humors which caused "the tooth-ache, cough, catarrhs, ear-ache, etc." No hats, in short, for the wards of the childhood reformers. Despite these medical warnings, elitist theories, and pedagogical points of view, 19th-century children continued to wear caps either because they were the offspring of farmers or because it was stylish to appear as if they were.

Colors as well as clothes suggested class, sex, occupation, and condition. Blue was a common color worn by school children, servants, apprentices, and poor people. Red, the color of kings and cavaliers, became popular when Rousseau, declaring that children liked bright colors, pointed out that red was the brightest of natural colors. For mourning, black clothes were prepared for all ages, typical accessories consisting of "a black Crepe Hatband, Black mourning Gloves, and Stockings and Shoe Buckles and 3 payres of black Buttons for wrist and neck." In the case of the death of a virgin, a child, or a woman lying-in, white often substituted as the color of death. White, of course, has an iconographic history of signifying purity, innocence, and holiness.

Low round-necked, high-waisted dresses in white, with full skirts straight to the ankle, set a Grecian mode for children of the 1780s. Petticoats were worn by boys as well as by girls, even though these garments were considered by many to be as unhealthy as stays, which had also been worn by both sexes until the age of six. By the 1790s, skirts were less full, the neckline square down to the short puffed sleeves. A decade later the style of having the neck and breasts bare in order to accustom girls to inclement weather was, according to Dr. Struve, of good intention but of bad consequence. The rest of the body being covered with warm clothes made the breast, in the good doctor's opinion, more susceptible to sickness. The reverse was equally damaging. Keeping the breasts too warm caused the common cold. Dr. Struve referred to the padded covering that warmed the breasts as "bosom friends" and added that they were unnecessary for healthy girls. Another mention of bosom friends appeared in a 1796 Philadelphia periodical, where they were described as pads or safeguards worn in bosoms during the cold weather. Included in the article is a warning that they are "scandalous" and "suspicious in appearance." Obviously, bosom friends were not merely chest warmers, but were the "falsies" of the 18th and 19th centuries. The author of the article, proper to a fault, recommended that girls use something more discreet for their "virgin zones."

The sash which accented the waistline at the end of the 18th century and at the beginning of the 19th was another fashionable hazard to good health, according to contemporary experts, although, if the dress were to consist of a short waist and sash, it merited consideration as the lifting relieved pressure and lessened the chances for coming down with the catchall disease of young people—rupture. Not being considered rational creatures, women were thought to have little resistance to old habits and prejudices. Consequently, such reformers of the national health as Dr. Struve, much like advertisers later in the 19th century and in our day who employed the threat of dire consequences to the health, used all their powers of persuasion to convince women to wear a dress all of one piece. The rules of true taste and propriety, Dr. Struve said, were never in opposition to those of health.

Chidren's clothing, like household government, carried with it into the new moderate 19th century a lingering moral residue of ambivalence towards children. Looser social ties, domestic protection, natural rather than willful piety, shame instead of brutality, and "nurture ruling nature" seemed to be the agents of control in the governance of children. Together, these exerted more civilized expressions of control than had been popular in previous centuries. Mathew Carey of Philadelphia observed in the child of the 19th century a happy balance which existed between indulgence and brutality—eighteen-year-olds were no longer whipped, and children no longer "vanished into the nurseries" or were given over entirely to hired servants. Parents were compassionate to their children and all siblings were equally entitled to inheritance before the law. Restraint, always present, had become, as far as possible, invisible. Catherine Beecher, in guiding parents to instill the three key tenets of childhood—"submission, self-denial, and benevolence"—suggested by the time of the American Civil War that household government be keyed to reward rather than penalties, to "love and hope in forming the habits of childhood."

27. *Ernesta with Nurse*, Cecilia Beaux, American, 1894. The wide-eyed innocence of this extraordinarily beautiful little girl indicates that the genteel could easily afford to let a child simply be a child, unlike the piously religious who still believed in the devil that had to be beaten out of it.

28. *Family Portrait*, artist unknown, American, 19th century.

2.

The Family and the Child

Images of childhood—in art, in literature, in the documents of any society in any period—may carry their own light weight in the history of civilization, but without the concept of "the family" as a backdrop, childhood studied by itself may be likened to a diaphanous curtain with nothing behind it to provide dimension. The idea of the family as a link in the divine Chain of Being, a link which functioned subordinately like other entities in this Western hierarchical notion of the universe, has existed at least since medieval days. But the nuclear or conjugal family—parents and children who stayed together for an extended period of time maintaining strong, close, and affectionate ties—did not always exist, and in fact did not often exist prior to 1600.

The family before the great age of reform was part of a larger network of marital units in the manorial system, directed more by the community than by single family groups. The family, then, according to Lawrence Stone's exhaustive study, *The Family, Sex, and Marriage,* was "an open-ended, low-keyed, unemotional, authoritative institution." In a rather mundane way the family began with a marriage that was not social, religious, or romantic. It was an economic union of bloodlines for purposes of inheritance, and it was a politically gathered group for self-protection in states that were weak and could not oversee their people. Marriage, like all life not spent in the cloister, was generally viewed as a concession to the flesh, a way to manage sin. The famous words of St. Paul—"It is better to marry than to burn"—were hardly taken lightly.

Every activity in medieval family life—labor, prayers, amusements, justice, and education—radiated not from the home and hearth, but from the manorial center under the direction of the lord of the manor. In the homes of middle and upper-class families, the concepts of privacy and individuality were completely unknown and, if ever dreamed of, were inherently impossible to put into practice since the household was often as large as thirty or forty people. In addition to parents and children, there were such legal, nonblood family members as servants, apprentices, boarders, and journeymen. Even clerks and bookkeepers lived-in. "It was a community in which all the members"—in Lawrence Stone's fine phrase—"lived in a perpetual crowd." And in a community without police, it was imperative that each man minded his neighbor's business. A sinful daughter and a pilfering son, for example, were of necessity the concerns of everyone.

Medieval family life had unique advantages for the young. Though families were not very cohesive, they were also not very demanding. Children quickly pushed themselves towards acceptance in the adult world, whether they worked and played at home, in the fields, or at the fair, and whether they went to church, feasted at the lord's manor after harvest, or left home for school and apprenticeship. The isolation, segregation, and protection of children which would eventually keep them innocent, and the adult intrusion, discipline, and regimentation of children which would eventually give them that nebulous quality called "character," were absent from medieval life. Children were left to grow up as fast as they could until the communal existence of medieval manors, town guilds, villages, monasteries, and collegiate church schools broke down under the heavy economic weight of land enclosures and the equally heavy weight of the humanistic conscience of the Reformation. The growing belief in self-realization, in individual glory, and in personal communication with God made the smaller family unit more inevitable, more important, more independent, and ultimately more controlling. Children, like other economic assets, took on new value for their families and new restrictions for themselves. "Modern" times surely brought with them mixed blessings.

Much of the extant information on early child-rearing practices comes from the surviving papers of English gentlemen who, focusing on family instead of community, first began seriously to collect self-centered documents on familial genealogy, heraldry, property, and ideology. This passion for collecting genealogical and antiquarian minutiae was predicated on the belief that divine blessing was somehow inherited along with property and coats-of-arms. These "ancient" family documents provided meet and proper evidence of a gentleman's distinction from the rest of mankind, children included. Because he wanted his distinctiveness made evident and visual, a gentleman, therefore, took the privilege of dressing children and other inferiors in the community differently from himself. "Correct" dress dictated that one could easily tell the degree and station of every man on sight. It was bad not to be dressed as well as one should but even worse to be overdressed and mistaken for a man of distinction. Consequently, King Charles in 1636 legislated against the sale or purchase of imitation jewelry, thus effectively keeping the adornments of the lower classes down to a minimum. When Quakers refused to doff their hats, this disorderly act was a visible blow to the universal belief in a hierarchy provided by God which implied a natural and necessary subordination of one class or entity to another that made the universe function. Any indication of disorderly attire, sometimes as simple as a child with one shoe off and one shoe on, had the effect of recalling a rebellious nature, the inheritance of Adam, that jeopardized authority.

Legislation was laid down to distinguish the classes, regulating not only types of clothing which could be worn, but amounts of food which could be consumed and

29. *The Streatfield Family*, William Dobson, British, 17th century. A deceased child is not only included in this portrait of an English Puritan family, but is decidedly its subject. As the mother, tenderly affected, points to the child (draped unlike the other family members), the father casts his eyes on a death's head resting upon a cracked column. The family's hopes lie with the surviving children, the younger of whom, like infants in every age, tugs at his father's clothes for attention.

kinds of sport which could be practiced by each. Archery, for example, was limited to the lower classes, and bowls and tennis were reserved for the wealthy. Physical punishment between the years 1500 and 1660 also followed class lines, being reserved for children on every social level and adults only of the working class. Even Puritans in early New England chose as leaders men whom God had already put on top. As one early American settler phrased it, "Honour, Submit to, and obey those whom God hath set over us; whether in family, church or Common-wealth."

The heads of the medieval family—the priest in the church and the lord of the manor—had been effectively replaced during the Reformation by the father of the children, the paterfamilias. The Protestant reformers, in short, brought new vigor to the status of the natural father. Without elegant clothes, lavish tables, or generous gift-giving—all previous signs of the elect in the ancient regime—the act of being a natural father, and of governing a group called "the household," became the only visible signs of the new elect. Father replaced, with unseen virtues of the heart, the old regime and public ritual of the early church. As the small Protestant sects grew in number and found themselves short of pastors, the paterfamilias emerged with new spiritual powers as the church in many ways became the home. What was at first intended as a

30. *Family at Tea*, artist unknown, Dutch, mid-18th century. With the tea table of this genteel 18th-century family set for two, the children—although dressed in the generation before Rousseau as miniature adults—are nonetheless excluded from the world of their elders.

temporary transfer of powers from the leaders of the sects to the heads of households became permanent and Father all important. He brought prayers in the house, and, consequently, grace to even the smallest child. As the Protestant leaders invested fathers with the power to pray and preach, they also invested homes as a sacred sphere where the art of the preacher could be practiced. The father, with such books as *The English Catechism Explained* tucked under his arm, was, by the third decade of the 17th century, "an epitome of the whole Gospel," a householder suddenly in charge of the eternal souls of his family.

The house, considerably changed from the day in which it was a hut, traveling entourage, or a monastery, grew with the importance of the role of the father into a more comfortable, more private, and still more spiritual place. The singing, playing, and socializing of all ages and sexes so characteristic of communal fairs was gradually subsumed by the privacy of the home, where family and children gathered in new cohesiveness, sharing a set of religious and social values that they called "the good life." Earlier accepted notions of what constituted "the good life," according to Lawrence Stone, had consisted of gentlemanly financial independence; the capacity to live idly without the necessity of undertaking manual, mechanical, or even professional tasks; and the ability to perform gracefully on the dance floor and on horseback, in the tennis court and the fencing school. But early Protestant families used as guidelines the vir-

31. *The Fondey Family*, Ezra Ames, American, 1803. If a century earlier death had dominated family portraits (figs. 16 and 29), it had by the end of the 18th century moved outside to the graveyard. Lest we miss the "presence" of the deceased, however, the family members gesture heavenwards and even the family dog looks upward. The name of the departed is included not only on the monument, but on the scroll at the upper right. Significantly, the mourning art that became fashionable in this period on both sides of the Atlantic concentrated on just such scenes as that formed in the background of this transitional portrait.

tues of thrift, service, literacy, labor, worship of God, and strict household government. In the 17th century the term *government* referred more often than not to all
family and church.affairs that were subject to the order of authority. As well as
mothers and their children, visiting friends, boarders, and sojourners were subject to
the increasingly strict family government.

Imparting "the good life" was an enormous responsibility for the father of the household and required him to provide food, instruction, correction, and spiritual inspiration to his wife, his children, his servants, his apprentices, and any living-in friends. It
was laid upon the men as fathers and employers to bring up the young in a virtuous occupation, for without a skill or a trade no child could become godly.

Books with such deadly titles as *A Godly Form of Household Government, The
Catechizing of Families, A Teacher of Householders, How to Teach Households, The
Plain Man's Pathway to Heaven, The Practice of Piety,* and *Of Domestical Duties*
were offered as religious guides to parents in the proper raising of children, one's own
as well as others'. The well-bred child was taught not only how to behave "at table,"
but to "wait at table," in the belief that making a child a good servant in the home
would also make him a good servant to God and his country. It is easy to see here the

32. *Family Group,* artist unknown,
American, c. 1805. Because folk art is
unhampered by such formalities as
correct perspective, it is frequently
spontaneous in its vision and direct in
its implications. Mother, who is at
least twice the size of father and who
dwarfs the diminutive little girl whose
hand she holds, dominates this
portrait just as she more than likely
dominated the life of the young girl
who painted it almost two
centuries ago.

expanding power of the paterfamilias—a power that developed from his semipriestly activities after 1640 and eventually nurtured a new kind of order in self-discipline, a new kind of independence in isolation, and a new kind of power in leading prayer. Once this authority, second only to God and king, was his, the Protestant father never again surrendered it to the church.

Just as fathers employed books on piety and household government to tame the spirit and prepare the soul, they also consulted etiquette manuals written for use at home to refine the habits of a boorish population of children and adults. It was the function of the father and the family to keep children "decent," by which was meant, among other things, to have clean hands, to urinate in secluded spots, to dress differently from adults, to keep one's legs uncrossed, and not to scratch, belch, or grind one's teeth in public, and to be "discreet" when spitting. Parents were responsible for the social order of the child whether he was at home, in the street, or traveling, since there were then no public authorities or institutions to curb anyone's unruly behavior. Only Hollywood epics give the false impression that the police have always been with us.

In each century, though family life had become less bestial, less dirty, less vulgar,

33. *Family Playing*, artist unknown, American, 19th century. This watercolor seems almost inspired by the words in *The Ladies' Garland* (1839): "A man finds at his own fireside satisfying enjoyments. He is exhilarated by the smiles of love, and the sports of juvenile gayety. After the toils of business . . . in the bosom of a beloved and affectionate family, he seeks and finds a sweet and refreshing repose."

and less disorderly, the need for manuals of etiquette continued to be used more as a child's reminder of familial duty than as a manual for ignorant or coarse citizens. The only real difference between early manuals and the later ones was one of style which progressed from dictatorial to entertaining and from direct to tactful. One of the more interesting books in this genre, *Memoirs of the Bloomsgrove Family*, published in Boston in 1790 and written in the guise of letters to a "respectable citizen," pleased 18th-century sensibilities in the new republic. It claimed that good manners benefitted children, especially girls, and promised on its elaborate title page that good manners equally benefitted the family, society, and the government of the United States of America as well. The author, Enos Hitchcock, a popular American follower of Rousseau, gently blamed the evils in his country on "the romantic ideas of elegance and splendor, borrowed from European writers, customs, and manners." He spent the larger portion of his book instructing females on their roles as good domestic managers. A wife had to be educated from childhood in the management of money. Too often, he thought, daughters were "born to expectations," to use the phrase of the day, and were therefore above learning the arts of domesticity. He cautioned boys in choosing a wife that "if she has no economy, he labors in vain."

34. *Maine Family*, artist unknown, American,
c. 1850. Although stiffly posed in the manner of a silhouette, this family scene is not without feeling. (Notice how the mischievous child seated at the left tickles the infant's foot.) Although it is impossible to know the sex of the three youngest children with certainty, the child in a dress and the seated mischief-maker are most likely boys because of their toys.

Although one can interpret the evolving history of the family through paintings, engravings, letters, diaries, sermons, etiquette manuals, and other visual and literary documents of centuries past, two of the most interesting approaches to understanding the nature of the family have been articulated in the modern era—one in the 18th century which defines families according to their moral values, and one in the 20th which categorizes families according to temperaments. Adam Smith, the 18th-century Scottish economist, posited two moral systems into which civilized society could be divided—"The loose system adopted by the people of fashion, and the strict or austere system, which is admired and revered by the common people and adopted by the wiser and better sort of the common people." In *The Protestant Temperament*, contemporary social historian Philip Greven devised self-explanatory views of family temperament—the genteel, the moderate, and the evangelical. Both approaches sug-

35. *Milinda Prouty Lamson and Her Son Nathaniel Lamson*, J. G. Chandler, American, c. 1842. By the 19th century a mother could no longer depend on swaddling or on a slat to support her infant's head and neck. Obviously aware of the delicacy of her baby's head, this mother cradles her child with great care. The baby, ungainly as most babies are, grasps his mother's finger as infants everywhere seem inclined to do.

gest that beneath the foundations of child-rearing practices rest the economic and social backgrounds of parents, set by material convenience and spiritual conviction. The loose morality of the people of fashion corresponds closely to the genteel mode of living, characterized visually in many of the illustrations in this book by fine clothing, elaborate toys, well-furnished houses, luxurious foods, good personal libraries, and many fine animals. The strict or austere moral values of the groups once thought "the wiser sort"—the yeomen, merchants, and succesful artisians—correspond closely to the evangelical expression of family temperament most often depicted in art by simple dress, the holding of bibles, the position of prayer, and attitudes of work. The propertyless farmer, the laborer, and the poor artisan seem to uphold Smith's austere system, revering morality but not necessarily adopting it.

The genteel classes were more willing to recognize than other groups the needs of the body and were of consequence obsessed with the outer self. They showed concern not only for the latest fashions and elegant establishments, but were often preoccupied with the joys of fine food and with the maintenance of good health. John Adams, describing the luxury he observed while breakfasting with friends in New York, noted

36. *Generations,* artist unknown, American, 19th century. These children properly affectionate, and respectful of their aged grandmother, exemplify the domestic ideal of Ralph Waldo Emerson: "Happy will that house be in which the relations are formed from character."

that "Mr. Scott has an elegant Seat there, with Hudsons River just behind his House, and a rural Prospect all round him. We satt in a fine Airy Entry, till called into a front Room to breakfast. A more elegant Breakfast I never saw—rich Plate—a very large Silver Coffee Pott, a very large Silver Tea Pott—napkins of the very finest Materials, and toast and bread and butter in great Perfection. After breakfast a Plate of beautiful Peaches, another of Pairs and another of Plumbs and a Muskmellon were placed on the table."

The concentration on fruit as a luxury is of interest here. Children of the well-to-do were often painted in portraits beside bowls of fruit or holding single apples, peaches, or luscious berries. Genteel children were also most often painted out of doors, or, if inside, sitting by an open window with the fresh air from the countryside blowing in. Like the respect John Adams showed for his friend's "rural Prospect" and "fine Airy Entry," there was confidence in country living and in its isolation. But the romantic appreciation of nature was by no means limited to the upper classes in Europe or North

37. *American Madonna and Child,* artist unknown, American, c. 1850. The 19th-century enthronement of motherhood, so exemplified by this beautiful portrait, found literary expression not only in the writings of such women as Catherine Beecher, but in such unlikely authors as Edgar Allan Poe: "The angels...singing unto one another, Can find among their burning terms of love, None so devotional as that of 'mother.'"

America. Fresh air became in the 19th century a panacea for religious, moderate, and evangelical families to curb and cure the world's spiritual ills. The magical qualities ascribed to country air were borrowed, of course, from the ancient pastoral writers of the Golden Age and their glorification of Nature and the simple life. Given the foulness of urban sanitation in every age, the retreat to rural Elysian fields was not without its practical side. Witness, for example, the prescription of James Nelson, English apothecary, in *An Essay on the Government of Children* (1768):

> To breathe in a free, open, pure Air, is undoubtedly of great Use; Children, therefore, especially if born in *London*, stand in need of this Assistance; they should have the Freedom of tasting a sweeter Air, than that which usually surrounds their Habitation.

The concerned apothecary, however, cautioned parents not to use clean air as an excuse for putting out the child to wet-nurse and rationalizing to their friends that their children were thriving better in the uplands.

38. *A Family Group*, artist unknown, British, mid-19th century. With the support of her husband, this woman, obviously the center of her family, is bringing up their children to conform to the words of the Psalmist that their "sons may be as plants grown up in their youth; their daughters as cornerstones, polished after the similitude of a palace." The portrait communicates 19th-century familial rectitude.

If parenthood in genteel families was a loving but distant relationship, with surrogate parents either in the child's home or in another home taking charge and often spoiling or corrupting the children, parenthood in the evangelical home was very responsible, direct, and even possessive. Under the pressure of trying to develop a kingdom of saints in the here and now, and knowing that childhood was the place to begin, the members of the "modern" family who came into direct contact with children—servants and possibly grandparents—were supervised by natural parents with vigor and suspicion. As sources of worldly influence, the caretakers of children were treated as beguiling conductors of sin who introduced vanity, gluttony, and sexual pollution to children, thereby impeding spiritual growth. Indulgent grandparents, in particular, were seen as potential problem-makers. As the minister John Robinson commented in 1620, "Children brought up with their grandfathers or grandmothers seldom do well, but are usually corrupted by their too great indulgence." John Wesley, in the late 18th century, reiterated similar injunctions to women raising children:

> Your mother, or your husband's mother, may be with you, and you will do well to shew her all possible respect. But let her on no account have the least share in the management of your children. She would undo all that you have done; she would give them their own will in all things. She would humor them to the destruction of their souls, if not their bodies too. Keep the reins in your own hands.

In genteel as well as in evangelical households, civility was the measure of success in a child's home education. Emphasis was placed on the importance of learning how to be sociable, how to be agreeable, how to carry on friendships, and how to gain reputation, respect, and virtue through proper conversation. Hugh Blair's *Lectures on Rhetoric*, one of the most respected texts of the 1750s, explained in its opening paragraphs why the discipline of conversation was so important:

> Speech is the great instrument by which man becomes beneficial to man; and it is to the intercourse and transmission of thought, by means of speech, that we are chiefly indebted for the improvement of thought itself.

Good taste in polite conversation, the employment of well-made sentences that were "perfectly happy and elegant," were yet another privilege of Calvinistic providence, another obvious separation that parents could teach at home. In manners of conversation, the well-bred youngster was exhorted to

Remember that the first rule is never to bring up frivolous matters among great and learned persons, nor difficult subjects among persons who cannot understand them. Do not talk to your company of melancholy things such as sores, infirmities, prisons, trials, war, and death. Do not recount your dreams. Do not give your opinion unless it is asked for. Do not attempt to correct the faults of others, especially as that is the duty of fathers, mothers, and lords. Do not speak before thinking what you intend to say.

Plus ça change, plus c'est la même chose.

Although the formal education of children is discussed elsewhere in this book, the very subject of education—in the past as now—cannot be divorced from a discussion of the nature of the family. Not everyone in the past, we should remember, was pleased to send his child to school, and, of course, not everyone could afford such a luxury if it was available. Beyond the objections of the farmer and workman who resented the time school took away from manual labor, there were objections from those who saw home and apprenticeship as the most valuable and civilizing experiences in the education of children. Many parents believed education at school destroyed a child's self-confidence and segregated him from the world of adults. A home education, they felt, taught him, as school never could, how his parents wanted him to behave. In 1661, for example, Maréchal de Cailliere wrote of family education:

39. *The Reverend John Atwood and His Family*, Henry F. Darby, American, 1845. This is a portrait of the quintessentially good evangelical family, with five bibles visible and with a biblical scene and a mourning picture decorating their Victorian parlor. The three daughters, knowing their proper place, sit upright and without emotion in the background. The expressionless faces of the family bear a similarity that goes beyond genetics.

It is not enough to be versed in the knowledge taught at school; there is another sort of knowledge which teaches how to use it...which speaks neither Greek nor Latin, but which shows us how to employ both. It is to be found in the Palaces, in the homes of Princes and grandees, it hides in the alcoves of ladies, it delights in the company of soldiers, and it does not despise merchants, laborers, or artisans. It has prudence as a guide, and its doctrines are conversation and experience.

But even those most in favor of home education recognized at least one possible snare: the greatest problem a home-bred child of genteel parents still had to face was the vulgar playfulness of servants, tutors, and other adults, a problem that did not disappear even for the evangelicals of the 18th and 19th centuries, who also commented wryly on it.

The family and the home were first celebrated in the 16th century. And it soon began to make its presence felt in art. In such texts as *Le Grand Proprietaire de toutes choses* (1556), a family group—including father, mother, and two sons—for the first time represented the ages or steps in the life of man instead of the usual singular figures employed in the past. Late medieval calendars that related particular months to particular human activities also featured the family, enlarging it to include daughters and servants, and depicting them at harvest in August, at the family meal in October, with the sick in November, or at the father's deathbed in December. The family as a fitting

40. *The Haight Family*, artist unknown, American, c. 1848. In sharp contrast to the Atwood family, the Haights display their learning—the fine arts, the literary arts, and the art of trade (geography)—as aspects of their wealth. Without the constraints of intense piety, this genteel family is free to enjoy a style of life that emphasizes their inner sense of self-regard and their immense pride.

subject for art increasingly moved from outdoor scenes to the intimacy of the home. The depiction of the birth of Mary, for example, was a pretext to illustrate the bedchamber of a home and an intimate family scene, subjects which undoubtedly fascinated the people of the 16th and 17th centuries. Privacy, something new, was rapidly becoming a major theme of painters who, well into the 19th century, illustrated kitchens, nurseries, and family parlors in genre and conversation pieces. Posed in the privacy of the parlor, family portraits frequently included deceased children, depicted as they has last been seen in the home, the only attribute to distinguish them from the rest of the family being an occasional cross, a death's-head, or a finger pointing up to the heavens.

By the late 17th century, life was being lived more fully by the modern family—and more and more within the confines of the house. There it was that people met one another as they might previously have done at church, at the fair, or at the pub. The houses of the rich of Western Europe, prior to the 17th century, consisted of a few very large rooms with a few windows on every floor. Great crowds of people inhabited them. Other houses were very small, with a room and sometimes two, a window and sometimes two, and a single floor and sometimes two. Engravings of the 16th and

41. *The Industrious Man,* from *Picture Lessons, Illustrating Moral Truth* (Philadelphia, c. 1850). The original 19th-century caption makes the moral message of this illustration clear: "It is Saturday night. The industrious man returns from his labour in peace. He is welcome to an humble home. Pleasant smiles and happy voices greet him. Let him fear and serve God and God will bless him and his household forever." Notice how a younger child is entrusted to the care of an older. But notice, too, that the working-class table, as in fig. 30, is still set for the two adults alone.

I. *Mary, Queen of Scots with Her Son James VI*, artist unknown, British, 16th century. Wearing an embroidered dress with sleeves under sleeves, a silken cap to match, gold necklace, and starched Venetian lace ruff, the baby James mirrors his royal mother's pride in physical beauty and great luxury.

II. *A Baptism*, attributed to Durs Rudy, Pennsylvania-German, c. 1825. For the family that believed in a kingdom of saints, the baptism of a child was of even greater significance than its birth. The quotation from Matthew 28 is a reference to the Trinity that became the vital content of Christian baptism after the Resurrection.

III. *Emma Van Name*, artist unknown, American, c. 1795. The littleness of childhood is suggested by the almost surreal proportion of the goblet of strawberries, the fruit sacred to the Virgin Mary and suggesting simultaneously innocence and ripeness. The child wears a phallic whistle of silver and coral to protect her from what was superstitiously believed to be evil designs of old women.

IV. *Girl Coming through a Doorway*, George Washington Mark, American, c. 1845. While the deathly images of a marble bust and an oil lamp hover almost imperceptibly in the room beyond, a young girl stands midway between darkness and light. Rarely have the tininess and the fragile insecurities of childhood been more evocatively portrayed.

V. *The Herbert Children*, Lambert Sachs, American, 1857. The loving responsibility of an older sibling for a younger, so avidly preached in didactic literature of the 19th century, is here illustrated. The infant, shoeless to indicate its lack of adult "civility," holds a barrel-shaped rattle.

VI. *Little Girl with Blond Hair,* artist unknown, American, c. 1830. The blond child wears clothing selected by a generation willing to please its children. Rousseau had written that the color red makes children happy, and contemporary physicians recommended laced shoes to keep them comfortable. There is no certainty, however, that the child is in fact a girl since, before the age of seven, both sexes were identically dressed.

VII. *Little Child with Big Dog,* William Mathew Prior, American, 1848. The necklace does not identify the child as a girl; such beads were worn by children of both sexes to avert the croup. On the contrary, the attributes of the child in blue—plumed hat, knife, whip, the large dog itself—suggest the strength, discipline, mischief, and command of a boy child.

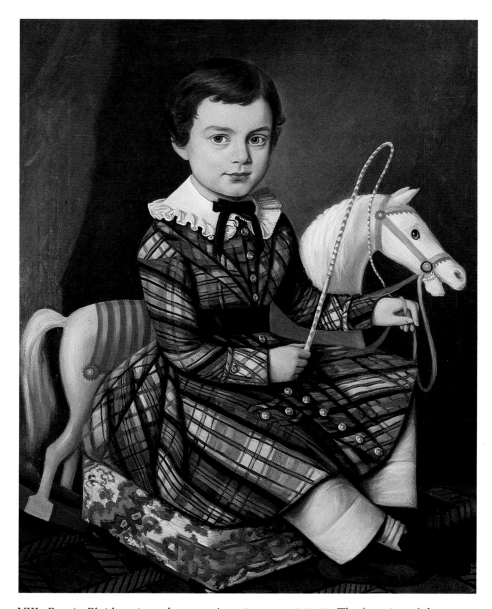

VIII. *Boy in Plaid,* artist unknown, American, c. 1840-50. The function of the hobby-horse is evident in an advertisement placed by a London cabinetmaker in the *Pennsylvania Packet* in 1785: "He makes Rocking-Horses in the neatest and best manner to teach children to ride and give them a wholesome and pleasing experience."

IX. *Carryl Children of Salisbury Center, New York,* artist unknown, American, 19th century. Although the stiffly-posed nature of this conversation piece almost makes the children appear to be objects among the other material goods of the Victorian parlor, the book, the hobby-horse and hoop, the whip and top and other toys suggest typical pastimes appropriate to the various ages of childhood.

X. *The Family at Home,* H. Knight, American, 1836. Although more relaxed than the previous illustration, this conversation piece is in its own way a reflection of 19th-century didacticism. According to the authorities of the day, the best way to establish a benevolent household was to surround the family with "amusing experiences" that instruct them in "industry, thrift, affection, and sympathy."

especially the 17th centuries often revolve around the common occasions of christening and marriage, emphasizing the social rather than the sacramental character of the events. These engravings illustrate the general socializing which took place in all the rooms—eating, drinking, dancing, and game playing. Even such suggestive little scenes as the first night of newlyweds were depicted unself-consciously in such early 17th-century engravings as the one done by Abraham Boose, entitled *The Newlyweds Go to Bed.*

Except for the kitchen, no room had its own particular function. Furniture was made to be folded and unfolded, for carrying from room to room and from house to house. Servants often slept next to their masters, allowing them to be more attentive to their employers' needs and enabling them at a moment's notice to fold away the beds for the day. In greater households the master's bed was sometimes stationary, with bed furniture or curtains that could be closed to provide the rare commodity of privacy. Since the bed, too, was placed in a public room where people gathered, bed furniture shielded from the public eye those who were asleep, in conjugal union, in childbirth, or dying. Such furniture was used as well in early American homes, where the business of living, as in the Middle Ages, was also a primitive social arrangement.

42. *The Happy Family*, from *Picture Lessons, Illustrating Moral Truth* (Philadelphia, c. 1850). "The happy family are on their way to the place of public worship. It is Sunday morning, and with neat attire and cheerful hearts they go up to the courts of the Lord." The rose-covered cottage, like the clothing of the common Christian family, is here obviously idealized. Their piety, however, is not. Such goodness, ironically, enabled the pious working man to toil in less than ideal circumstances with little or no complaint.

Seventeenth-century New England interiors were furnished much the same as were English houses of the period and included trestle tables, benches, a single chair for the head of the household, some table linen, knives but no forks, dishes, trenchers, earthenware, beakers, bowls, cups, salts, and many sizes and numbers of chests and boxes that served as the early containers for clothes. Stools, bedsteads, beds (or what are now called mattresses), chamber pots, sometimes a table, and less often a carpet for the table, were also listed in household inventories of both countries. Due in part to primitive heating conditions and in part to social attitudes about family living, only the hall—usually the one large room on the first floor—was furnished for regular family use all year long. The hall was, in fact, the only place for living, for cooking, for work- ing, sleeping, relieving oneself, washing, and receiving friends. With the typical English and American family confined in a house that did not accommodate the separation of functions, both public and private, and with that family of all ages and conditions living together for most of the year in one large room, the need for good habits and for adhering to the rules of etiquette seemed essential to make life workable, bearable, and possible. Under these physical and psychological conditions the desire to inculcate pious or moral behavior and develop well mannered children seems hardly unreasonable. Domestic peace and child rearing must have been very real and repressive struggles, indeed.

43. *Family Scene*, Walter Granville Smith, American, c. 1890. The artist has captured a moment of shared intimacy between parents and children in a genteel family of the Gilded Age—with son drawn to mother, and daughter to father. Despite the obvious affection, the children are nonetheless visitors to the world of adults, permitted a few minutes therein before they return once again to the safety and isolation of their own quarters. Notice how the table, set for two, serves as a motif for the segregation of children into a separate class.

It took the 18th century to build houses for individuals, structures that would not only allow families to withdraw from the outside world but would allow individuals to withdraw from one another—houses with corridors, where people did not have to pass one another each time they left or entered the room; houses with bedrooms and other rooms that had specific functions. Special quarters with bells were devised so that servants could be housed separately from the family and summoned when needed. And children, the "innocent ones," could finally be isolated from everyone. In an environment that moralists had been seeking since the end of the 16th century, parents could finally respond to the pleas of modesty which were written into many manuals of household government:

A Mother should by no means appear too much undressed in the Presence of her Son; nor a Father in that of his Daughter; for these and many other things, though in themselves innocent . . .give Boys a Boldness which borders on Impudence; and they are apt to wean Girls from some Degree of that Modesty they ought so carefully to preserve.

In the building of homes to accommodate privacy, the Victorian ethic of modesty was born.

44. *Helping Grandpa,* artist unknown, American, 19th century. Such popular magazines as *The American Agriculturist* exhorted 19th-century children to behave thoughtfully toward their grandparents in their "twilight years." But despite the warnings from reformers that grandparents tend to spoil children, the popularity of this sentimental theme in literature and in art underscores the axiom that every generation revolts against its fathers and makes friends with its grandfathers.

45. *Girl with Toys,* from *Children's Delight* (Boston, 1889).

3.

The Child at Play

When John Gratton was ten years old and playing vigorously with friends, or "frolicking" as the 17th century would have called it, he met the Lord:

> The Lord visited me with the light of his Son, and gave me to see the vain life and way I lived in being much given to play amongst rude boys, and took great delight in playing at cards, and shooting at butts, and ringing of bells.... I came to see that vain sports and pleasures were displeasing to the Lord.

The Gratton boy's rejection of pleasure, his condemnation of play, and his guilt from having experienced "delight" were part and parcel of his inheritance of the American Puritan conscience, a pious attitude that rejected the vulgar playfulness of the medieval past. Looking back, the reformers of the 17th century saw a gaming, drinking, reveling crowd, like the tentacles of some sinful octopus, reaching out to engulf their children. In an effort to restore a more saintly state for young ones and for everyone, fathers and clergymen set out to restrain play and separate the generations, hoping to destroy evil by isolating it like some dread disease.

The medieval community, against which John Gratton's generation had rebelled, enjoyed the exercise of games, the competition of sports, and the frivolity of toys. Regarded neither as mere childish pursuits nor as a waste of time, amusement was not only a completely natural part of life itself, but was very much a communal exercise. Amusement was seasonal, social, and religious, the culmination of a year's work and the celebration of a community of lords, yeomen, peasants, bailiffs, vagabonds, men, women, old people, and young children enjoying themselves in one wild crowd. Play was integral to all aspects, religious and otherwise, of popular fairs and harvest festivals, of Twelfth Night, Christmas Eve, and All Souls Eve. Such celebrations as May Day allowed for a break in the normal medieval hierarchical order and permitted females to express momentary equality with males as they played aggressively and provocatively, chasing them on "the stang" or hobby-horse and beating them with birch rods. And little boys caused violent disruptions in the psalm-singing parades or by becoming drunk with their fathers at the feasting tables. These medieval celebrations glorified the fruits of a man's labor and intensified the sense of community with men and of man's partnership with God. Revelry and merriment were considered among the tangible benefits and pleasures for all and were the logical conclusions of a divine contract in an age of faith untroubled by the restraints of Calvinism. Each medieval man, unlike the generations that followed, gave his child as much access to entertainment as to the work of the day.

46. *St. Dorothy*, artist unknown, German, 15th century. According to Christian legend, a young angel was sent to fulfill the wish of the Roman Theophilus who had sarcastically requested that the martyred Dorothy send him some flowers from Paradise "when she got there." That the heavenly child should be portrayed riding a down-to-earth hobby-horse is one of the surprises and delights of medieval art.

Games and sports for children were exercises in living rather than mere relaxation from life. Henry Peacham, writing in *The Compleat Gentleman* in 1622, espoused the peculiarly modern belief that sports were a form of communication between father and son or master and student. In the 15th century the genteel child was trained to hunt, hawk, ride, and joust. The seasons of the chase were marked by religious holidays, the fox being hunted between the Nativity and the Annunciation, the roe between Michaelmas and Candlemas, the hart from Michaelmas to Midsummer, and the boar from the Nativity to the Purification of Our Lady. The hunt and other forms of physical exercise provided the essential education (and sometimes virtually the only education) a young gentleman received, since reading was usually left to the "children of meaner people." The use of the bow, the sling, and the spear acquainted all boys with the skills of the soldier and gave them the exercise which made them strong enough to do a man's work. Common children, however, learned to master more brawling sports—that is, how to wrestle, to swim, to play skittles, and to bowl. Although tennis was the sport of nobles, shuttlecock (or battledore) and billiards were

47. *Merry Company on a Terrace,* Jan H. Steen, Dutch, c. 1670. There was a time when children were freely included in the world of adults at play and were at the least participatory witnesses of every form of human revelry. In the years following the late 17th century, children were increasingly segregated from adult pleasures in all but the lowest classes.

played by "the meaner" children. Eventually rough ball games were abandoned by upper-class adults and relegated to children or to the lower classes in general. If one is to accept on faith the testimony of most literature before the Reformation, almost everyone enjoyed singing and dancing—the adults, the children, the nuns, the monks, the wet nurses, and their infant charges.

In those days of communal entertainment, children and adults alike played such running games as cat-after-mouse, hide and seek, blindman's buff, and leapfrog. In later centuries, when social stratification had become more pronounced and the upper and middle classes segregated themselves in work and private play, the poor still gathered in front of their houses on Sunday to play hopscotch and leapfrog, to jump in sacks, climb greasy poles, roll wheelbarrows blindfolded, and to drink. Like their medieval counterparts, laborers' children in later centuries drank publicly with their families, behaving, as one observer expressed it, "as happy as pigs in muck." Thus, long after the Calvinistic paterfamilias and the upper classes turned their backs on unabandoned play, lower-class children and adults remained free to have their fill of sensual pleasure. Unsegregated from adults and unprotected from society, poorer children played longer in the streets, unaware of the doors confining other children within four walls as the family grew more "private."

Like other facets of child rearing, the kinds of amusement encouraged by parents depended largely on the degree of education, social status, and even piety of the fami-

48. *Childhood*, Abraham Bosc, French, 17th century [reproduced from *Jeux* (Paris, 1900)]. While an infant in its cradle is teased by a mischievous boy and a very young child is restrained in its pen from crawling on the floor, the older children play with dolls or with marbles. The panels picturing God and the creation of Adam remind the viewer that children are natural heirs of original sin.

ly. Early aristocratic parents had relied on the hunt as an important aspect of the nurture of boys, a sport practically synonymous with the state of being a gentleman, and one which was not at all inconsistent with Christian practice. Although gentlemen of the old regime had no doubts about a life of leisure, many Protestants questioned whether the traditional gentlemanly code—the rejection of the gospel of work—stood in contradiction to the Christian message. They also resisted as impious the passion a gentleman felt for such bloody field sports as the hunt and shooting, which differed from hunting in that it was a private affair rather than a public chase. Although the camaraderie of man and animal is not always easily grasped in modern times, the hounds and the horses, essential to these gentlemanly and masculine field sports, seemed almost to join the hunter in an unspoken partnership in nature and in the joy of the fields. According to their aristocratic masters, in fact, hounds did not bark—they spoke. And indeed they appear to be "speaking" in the hundreds of extant portraits of gentlemen's sons and their hounds, loyal to one another and well trained. These almost stereotypical portraits of the "education" of a young aristocrat were revered and recopied until the nature of the gentleman was eventually altered by social reform. Then the boy and his dog, remnants of a sport now deemed decadent and wasteful, continued to be illustrated in the pictorial arts as demonstrations more of love and affection in middle-class families than of partnership and membership in a closed society.

It was difficult in any century but the 18th and the 20th for a pious or "industrious"

49. *Toyshop*, Fortier-Marotte, French, 18th century. By the late 18th century, toyshops catered to the tastes of the wealthy by providing opulent playthings for their offspring, including ingeniously-contrived *androides*, mechanical figures that simulated the actions of human beings. Compare the elegance of this French toyshop with the simplicity of play recommended by Rousseau and pictured in the illustrations following.

person to sanction the sendentary games of cards, dice, and chess. These pastimes were regarded by Puritans and Quakers as a waste of good time and, even in medieval days, as the work of the devil. As far as possible, they were kept away from young apprentices and clergymen because to depend on chance was to doubt the divine order of God. George Whitefield, one of the many clergymen disturbed by such ungodly "disorder," preached to 18th-century Englishmen and Americans that "cards, dancing, and such like, draw the soul from God."

Although it was difficult to legislate against dancing, attending plays and circuses, or reading novels, these activities, which stirred the imagination towards "undependable passions," were regarded with great suspicion. Such intense moralists as Quaker founder George Fox denounced the evils not only of feasts and games of all sorts, but the equally pernicious effects of the sedentary and worldly pursuits of reading and spectator sports. In order to discourage the gamesters from settling in Pennsylvania in 1682, a "Great Law" was passed forbidding "such rude and riotous sports and practices as Prizes, Stage-plays, Masques, Revels, Bull-baiting and Cock-fighting." In 1705 the Pennsylvania Assembly regulated tavern behavior by forbidding the playing of "cards, dice, shovel-board, billiards, ninepins, and any other kind of game whatsoever, now invented or hereafter to be invented."

Seventeenth-century reformers objected to what they considered the cruelty of the circus, the vanity of plays, and the unreality of puppets. They were joined in the late

50. *Butterflies*, artist unknown, French, 18th century [reproduced from *Jeux* (Paris, 1900)]. James Nelson's *Essay on the Government of Children* (1768) was lavish in its praise of physical exercise for children. Following the lead of Rousseau, Nelson wrote that "Exercise affords the most natural and the most comfortable Warmth to our whole Frame that can be. Exercise makes the Blood and other Juices circulate with Freedom . . . ."

18th century by physicians who believed that puppet shows were contemptible and corrupting influences which destroyed "every sense of symmetry and beauty" and were "peculiarly hurtful at any age when the talent of distinguishing between incongruity and propriety is not yet formed." If Punch and Judy had their backs to the wall, the ubiquitous street magician fared even less well. Such Quakers as John Woolman soon "exposed" a similar deceit in the idle diversion of legerdemain.

Even the pleasures of eating were soon to be subjected to willful scrutiny by the Methodist John Wesley. "Next to self-will and pride," Wesley exclaimed, "the most fateful disease with which we are born, is *love of the world.*" Therefore, he insisted, parents who *"enlarge the pleasure of tasting"* invited passions that unsettled the character. Or as historian Philip Greven has paraphrased Wesley: "To discipline the palate and to govern the stomach [are] important elements in shaping character." In one way or another, most of these reformers believed that the fun, the surprise, the mystery, and the passions of life were not to be entirely forgotten, but were to be reinvested in God, and were not to be lost to games or gluttony, but to be exercised by working for the perfection of the universe in man. The Englishman Robert Barclay, therefore, listed amusements which he thought were "more favorable" to God than field sports or sedentary games—such useful pastimes as conversations with Christians, the reading of history books, gardening, visiting friends for tea, and tinkering with scientific and mathematical instruments. Indeed, botany and science were particularly suitable hobbies for American Quakers. Without doubt, the life of play for the children of evangelical and reformed Christians was tepid tea at best and "Christian conversation" at the very least.

Toys—those objects that the modern mind conceives of being made especially for children—were originally very limited in number, type, and place of purchase. In medieval times toys were obtained seasonally when craftsmen brought them to religious and community festivals. Otherwise children played on the floor with the household animals, with the food in the kitchen, the vagabonds on the street, and the tools in the workshop. Because children were not particularly distinguished from adults by the medieval mind, toys were not made especially for children any more than nursery rhymes or riddles were written for them. According to some authorities, in fact, only rhyming alphabets and lullabies were originally meant for the nursery.

The hoops and the hobby-horses, the marbles and the birds on sticks—toys occasionally pictured in medieval illuminations—were toys for everyone at the seasonal festivals. Hoops were acrobatic props also used by the dancers in traditional musical presentations. The hobby-horse and other early toys, historians would have us believe, were not without their symbolic meanings and origins. The horse, a symbol of power and maleness belonging to boys, was vicariously enjoyed by women and girls during public celebrations. The wooden bird on a stick, derived from ancient Greek custom, survived its pagan origins as a feature of a Christian spring festival dedicated to youth, birth, fruitfulness, innocence, and the Holy Spirit. The bird on a stick, like birds in a cage or tied to a leash, symbolized the limitations of childhood and of human life on earth.

The toy market first accommodated the English noble class in the 17th century, at just about the time that childhood became generally accepted as a world all its own. Childhood, as one of the ages of man, was given popular recognition when books written expressly for children—the *Orbis Pictus* of John Amos Comenius (the first textbook with pictures adopted for the teaching of children), John Bunyan's *Book for Boys and Girls*, and James Janeway's *A Token for Children*—came into the marketplace. The list of toys given to the future king of France, Louis XIII, when he was a baby suggests the range of items that could have been purchased by the rich in 1601: a hobby-horse, a windmill, a whipping top, a tambourine, soldiers, a cannon, a tennis racket, a ball, a clockwork pigeon, scissors, cutting paper, and dolls (male only). At four the future king was practicing archery, playing cards, playing racket ball, and joining in

51. *Cherry Candy*, artist unknown, French, 19th century [reproduced from *Jeux* (Paris, 1900)]. Dressed in the skeleton suits and the loose-fitting dresses recommended by the followers of Rousseau, these children are playing outdoors with objects drawn from nature itself. In addition to the game with cherries illustrated, they would have also played "cherry pit" by tossing cherry stones into a small hole in the ground.

such parlor games as fiddle-de-dee, hand-clapping, and hide and seek. At six he played chess, trades, charades, and pantomime. At seven—that transitional age when he would no longer be educated by women—he was forbidden to play with dolls and soldiers, and the skills of riding, hunting, fencing, shooting, and gambling replaced his toys. He continued, however, to play such games as blindman's buff, I-sit-down, and hide and seek, since they, too, were a part of the adult world.

By the 18th century toy shops had sprung up in small towns all over Europe to cater to a middle-class public enjoying the new taste of little indulgences that once belonged only to the genteel. Spoiled children, easy to identify at play, were sometimes the cause of great irritation to the moderate or evangelical man—such as the gentleman who, at the time the following letter was reprinted in the *Virginia Gazette* in 1767, was on his way home to England after a disappointing visit with friends in America:

> On my arrival here I found a house full of children, who are *humoured* beyond measure, and indeed absolutely spoiled by the ridiculous indulgence of a fond mother . . . . Six of the children are permitted to sit at the table, who entirely monopolize the wings of fowls; and the most delicate morsels of every dish . . . . In the morning, before my friend is up, I generally take a turn upon the gravel walk, where I could wish to enjoy my own thoughts without interruption; but I am here instantly attended by my little tormentors, who follow me backwards and forwards, and play at what they call *Running after the Gentleman*. My

52. *Scenes from a Seminary for Young Ladies* (detail), artist unknown, American, 1810-20. In 1801 Joseph Strutt described the universal pastime of skipping rope in the following manner: "Skipping—This amusement is probably very ancient. It is performed by a rope held by both ends and thrown forward or backwards over the head and under the feet alternately." Its place as an exercise taken by young schoolgirls is wonderfully captured in this rare watercolor, most likely executed by a student herself.

whip, which was a present from an old friend, has been lashed to pieces by one of the boys, who is fond of horses; and the handle is turned into a hobby horse . . . . Once as an amusement for the evenings, we attempted to begin reading *Tom Jones*, but were interrupted, in the second page, by little *Sammy*, who is suffered to whip his top in the parlour . . . . It is whispered in the family that . . . I cannot *talk to children*.

For many families the concern with boisterous children playing with toys was replaced by a protective alertness to the dangers of toys. Doctors were beginning to caution parents about playthings made of plaster of Paris, clay, glass, and porcelain; of small trumpets and whistles; and of toys and confectionaries painted with poisonous colors. Children then as now were creatures of the senses and sampled all objects with their tiny mouths. The technology of toy making was paralleled by new health concerns and affectionate respect developing in parents for their children. The end of the

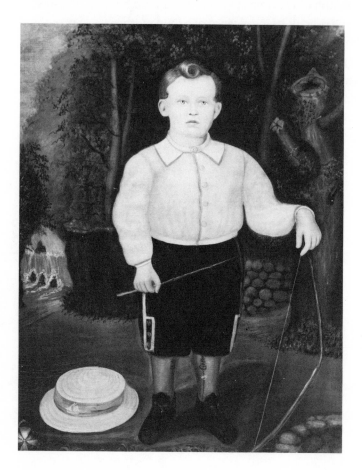

53. *Portrait of John William Larner*, artist unknown, American, 19th century. Young Master Larner is portrayed as the stereotypical male child of the 19th century. Wearing the breeches that set his age as above six or seven and a hat rather than the bonnet of early childhood, he pursues archery and ball playing, both acceptable pastimes for young males.

18th century was characterized by a willingness of parents to be close to their children, brought on in part by greater confidence in infant survival and in part by the educational theories of John Locke and Jean Jacques Rousseau that had become fashionable and popular. Although the two philosophers differed widely in their opinions on the influence of intruding parents and in the value of instructional toys, both men agreed that children were not born evil and that play was not signalling sin. Many moderate parents, believing that children began life in a state close to perfection, responded positively to new toys, games, and amusements, joining the genteel in a relaxation of their pious criticisms.

Posing with their children in a conscious preservation of the new educated sentiment of family and of child, parents of the middle and upper classes—genteel, moderate, and pious alike—employed artists to paint "conversation pieces" and genre scenes of the conjugal group. Some families were depicted playing together on swings, walking with animals, flying kites, sitting in the park, fishing, dancing in the parlor, or seesawing. Others were pictured attending plays, reading books, and eating at the breakfast table or gathering for tea. These family portraits reveal that, by 1800, young children were dressed differently from their parents and treated differently from adults in general, even though we know that after the rite of passage they were expected to turn

54. *William C. Wilson and Eliza K. Wilson,* artist unknown, American, c. 1860. The sexes of the young siblings are determined by their playthings. The boy holds a whip and rides his rocking horse, while his sister looks on passively and holds a flower. The ostensibly educational function of the rocking horse is explained in plate VIII.

out to be exactly the same as their elders—little chips, as it were, off the old blocks. In contrast to ambisexual clothing which neutered the children, toys and attributes of sport were often the only distinguishing features in these family portraits identifying the sex, age, and, occasionally, the temperament of the child. The hobby-horse, the whip or cane, the knife, the arrow, the gun, the large dog, the watch, the drum, the whipping top, and marbles were signs—remnants of medieval life—of the man to be and the gentleman. Dolls, needle and tinsel work, trinkets, and sedentary games were the main attributes of little girls. Birds, a sign of the spirit, often represented a holy—that is, deceased—child.

Of necessity, any survey of young children at play has to be pieced together from the few extant child-rearing records in personal diaries; from many pages of contemporary advice by such philosophers as John Locke and Jean Jacques Rousseau; from the writings of such physicians as M. Heroard, King Louis XIII's doctor, and Christian Augustus Struve; and such apothecaries as James Nelson; from the books of such women as Catherine Beecher, Hannah Moore, and Sarah Pierce; from the pages of such pioneering 19th-century researchers as Alice Morse Earle and Joseph Strutt; from the current scholarship of historians Philippe Aries, Lawrence Stone, Philip Greven, James Obelkevich, John Demos, and J. William Frost; and from the iconographic or symbolic inferences observed in paintings of children and in other illustrations of childhood. The last, one of the prime concerns of this book, has an immediacy that happily cuts across centuries to bring together the evidence of both historical documents and modern scholarship. Through an understanding of the child in art, we can learn much about the state of children in society in any age.

The paintings of royal children of the 16th and 17th centuries reveal a parental wish for instant and premature adulthood. The distance and formality of their public lives was more acceptable in portraiture than the ribaldries of the nursery or the court. Affection is absent in both family portraits and in those of a boy and his horse or his hound. These portraits of mother and child or boy and horse are very much like the contract of marriage, an arrangement of partners without strong signs of affection and companionship.

The paintings of genteel children of the 18th century, however, portray a note of genuine affection between parents and children and between children and animals. Soft cuddly pets—dogs, cats, and lambs—appear often in the laps of children. Held close to the body, these creatures become signs of love in the family and signs of age in the child. One had to be under seven to be free to enjoy a sensual nature. Before that age, the child was effeminate and therefore able to indulge in hugging and touching. Visual signs of affection would end for the child in his "age of reason"—after seven.

The poor and the pious child, depicted in art with their animals, show the effects of labor and of religion on their lives more than of affection and play. Poor children, of course, *worked* with animals, herding sheep and feeding chickens, for example. Pious children are portrayed learning moral lessons from their animals—of responsibility, of sympathy, and of benevolent action. The moral stories in the 19th-century pictures are not always obvious unless, as in some illustrated books and magazines of the Victorian period, the message is printed below the scene. Such annotations, ensuring the didactic point, are often graphic evidence of 19th-century pious intrusion. Entitled "Take Your Choice," one illustration of a gentle-looking mother with a lap full of kittens and two young children leaning over them, turns out not to be a study of family affection or of benevolence towards helpless animals, but a cold and pointed tale of a death-making decision to be made by a boy of five or six years. Though the other child in the picture is the elder of the two, she is a girl—tender-hearted and incapable of such "reasonable" choices—and responsibility rests with the boy, therefore, to decide which little kitten will be lucky enough to live. Such "moral" instruction through the joy of reading was

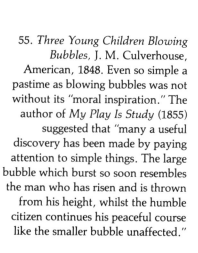

55. *Three Young Children Blowing Bubbles*, J. M. Culverhouse, American, 1848. Even so simple a pastime as blowing bubbles was not without its "moral inspiration." The author of *My Play Is Study* (1855) suggested that "many a useful discovery has been made by paying attention to simple things. The large bubble which burst so soon resembles the man who has risen and is thrown from his height, whilst the humble citizen continues his peaceful course like the smaller bubble unaffected."

56. *Take Your Choice*, from a
painting by Lilly M. Spencer,
American, 1869. Children were
expected to draw moral lessons even
from their play with animals. What
appears to be a Victorian illustration
of great sentiment is actually a choice
being made as to which of the litter of
kittens will be spared from
death by drowning.

57. *The Firecracker*, D. F. Bigelow, American, 1850. This scene of disarray suggests that the intermingling of children and adults at play was not entirely lost in the Middle Ages, but survived in poorer families through later centuries. The children have been playing with common household objects: paper, quill pens, a knife, a watering can, an apple peeler. The peaceful checkers game will soon be disrupted by the blast of a firecracker, suggesting the chaos that can result from the absence of adult restraint.

58. *New Year's Eve*, F. Fuchs, American, c. 1865. On New Year's Eve a group of children stand before a toyshop anticipating the joys of the morrow. As late as the early 20th century, gifts were traditionally exchanged on New Year's Day rather than on Christmas, a German practice that eventually prevailed in America. As one observer wrote in 1912, "New Year's gifts still pass generally from friend to friend and between members of a family."

the tactful, if not the unctuously tacky, way the 19th century went about imparting spiritual guidance to its young. But at least the sensibilities of the childish mind were finally receiving the same attention as weakness in the childish body.

By the 19th century, dolls, doll clothing, elaborate doll houses, and toy soldiers were mass produced for English and American parents who were buying these and other "frivolous" items for their youngsters. In addition, such "instructive" toys as jigsaw puzzles, travel games, and cards were also available for purchase. A century earlier, booksellers had offered educational playing cards to the public. These cards both amused and instructed children in the first steps of music, geography, spelling, and correct pronunciation, and a discount was given to boarding schools that made sizable purchases. Children became a ready market for entrepreneurs selling "good toys"—"Moses baskets" simulating the one that saved the life of the famous biblical infant, baa lambs and squeaky pigs imitating the joys of the open countryside, and

59. *The Young Architect,* from *The Nursery* (1875). The game of dominoes (called *cards* or *stones* in England and *men* or *pieces* in America) could be played in such variations as Matador, Sebastopol, Domino Loo, Malahoff, Cypress, Round the Clock, and many others. This small child, however, has invented his own game and is using the dominoes as building blocks. Even very restrictive parents would have approved of this "practical" use of an otherwise "wasteful" pastime.

musical instruments representing the more cultivated arts. Medical advisers of the day suggested toys that could be put together and taken apart, erected and destroyed—card houses, dominoes, or building blocks. According to the best sources, toys that could be "used"—drums and hobby-horses, for example—were better than dolls at which children "could only stare."

Maria Edgeworth, the popular 18th-century English writer of moral stories for children, agreed with those who objected to useless toys. She proposed the universal availability of mechanical toys for boys—water mills, looms, inflatable globes, perspective views, toy theaters, and camera obscuras—toys that would prepare little boys for the practical world. Jean Jacques Rousseau, Maria Edgeworth's inspiration and the man whose theories brought worldwide attention to the particular conditions of children, flatly denied any value, spiritual or otherwise, to the teaching of children

60. *Building Blocks*, from a German-American magazine, c. 1880. Building blocks were among the most popular of Victorian toys. A contemporary advertisement (1879) hailed their great utility: "Building blocks are among the most pleasing and instructive toys ever invented for children. The structures provide many happy hours for boys and girls, do not readily fall apart, and can be handled and carried about. Children do not soon become tired of the blocks, as their ingenuity is constantly being called into exercise."

until they were over twelve. He concluded that nature provided a child with his best toys, as it did his imaginary pupil Émile. Orphaned, rich, noble, strong, and reared in a rural environment, Émile was Rousseau's sanctified child, educated by his natural environment as he exercised in the fresh, pure air or in the cold, wet weather as he dug in the earth to plant, and as he derived his pleasures from the efforts of work:

> Let him work or let him amuse himself; both are the same to him. His games are his tasks, he feels no difference. He puts in everything he does an interest which makes one laugh and a liberty which pleases. . . . Is it not the spectacle of this age, a sweet and charming spectacle, to see a pretty child, his eye frank and laughing, and doing, as he plays, the most serious things, or profoundly occupied with the most serious amusements?

The words of Rousseau were echoed in America by Emerson and Thoreau, Whitman and Beecher. Parents, in consequence, attempted to be more respectful of childhood, and children in turn were allowed to be more "natural" than ever before. Portrait painters began to pose children with garden tools, baskets of flowers, bowls of fruit, and such common animals as squirrels, dogs, cats, and chickens. Nature's gifts, always having been signs of the generosity of divine providence or of family sanctity, were now understood in portraits of children as symbols of parents properly educated

61. *In the Park*, source unknown, American, c. 1879. Children's play was strictly categorized by sex: girls, dressed as young matrons in the 1870s, were permitted to practice for eventual motherhood with dolls and carriages; boys, wearing the military caps imitated from Civil War uniforms, were allowed more rigorous playthings.

to produce the "good" child that Rousseau described. Under his direction the child was to be regulated by nature's rules, learning to dig and plant and to derive enjoyment from the property he produced—which only then rightfully belonged to him. Physical exercise, Rousseau claimed, hardened the child's muscles and prepared him in the best possible way for mature sorrow, for all ailments, and for the strengthening of his soul. Accordingly, Rousseau approved of gymnastic exercises and swimming, although he found horseback riding a useless sport. The acceptable games for boys were the same to him as those for men—tennis, billiards, archery, and football. Playing blindman's buff, which accustomed children to the dark, was good for the same experiential reason that mild burns accustomed children to fire, and Rousseau, accordingly, recommended both. Girls, he thought, could benefit from working in the garden, and also from flying kites.

62. *Palo Alto Spring,* Thomas Hill, American, 1878. Amusement for the genteel on a warm spring day might have consisted of watching the younger members of the family participating in a game of croquet. Ten years before this painting was executed, *The American Agriculturist* recommended the pastime to farm families for the following reasons: "It is one of the few outdoor games which both sexes can share. The exercise is gentle and facilitates rather than hinders conversation. It is a pleasant relaxation for young and old." But whether rural children took readily to this upper-class English export is doubtful.

Rousseau was not the only thinker who attributed ultimate value to exercise and fresh air for children. Many contemporary physicians believed that sickness was caused by a "corrupted" atmosphere. As Dr. Christian Augustus Struve wrote in his *Domestic Education of Children* (1802):

Persons who have been remarkable for health and longevity, have uniformly spent the greatest part of their lives in the open air. Even the power of vision may be improved or impaired. . . . Many persons who live in the narrow lanes and streets of town, are afflicted with weak eyes: the cause of such complaints must be attributed to the want of a pure atmosphere. . . . We cannot bestow greater benefits on our children, than by exposing them frequently and daily to the enlivening influence of fresh air . . . under the canopy of heaven . . . inhaled, as it were, from the bosom of Nature. In large towns, young people should be sent to open and green fields [to] public places devoted to the exercise and recreation of children . . . and divert themselves by running about and playing upon the grass.

With sickness added to the moral suspicions already cast on cities by late 18th-century philosophers, physicians, and theologians—despite the fact that cities produced the bulk of the toys, the furniture, the clothing, and the books intended for children—it is not surprising to find most 19th-century thinkers continuing to glorify the rural life. Such popular writers as the Englishwoman Hannah More and the American writers and school mistresses Sarah Pierce and Catherine Beecher continual-

63. *Ship-Building*, Winslow Homer, American, 1873. Although Wordsworth may have been metaphorically correct in declaring that "the child is father of the man," these children—playing literally in the shadows of their fathers—demonstrate that in the choice of occupation, through the 19th century at least, the father was most definitely father of the child.

ly "spiritualized" the outdoors, Sarah Pierce recommending as rewards for good behavior not toys or orange cake which would inspire greed and gluttony, but "a visit with an animal" or a day in the garden. In her book *The American Woman's Home* (1869), Catherine Beecher alerted women to their responsibility for the physical, spiritual, and recreational health of the family. The only legitimate amusement she could envision was the preparation of the body for the discharge of duty. Any recreation which interfered with work, induced fatigue, wearied the mind, or replaced time for sleep was sinful. It was a woman's duty to see that household stoves, furnaces, and chimneys were built to provide not only heat, but "scientific domestic ventilation" as well. The proper motivation for "domestic exercise" was a third important female responsibility. If such exercise as walking was good, then exercise which interested the mind—such as walking to meet a friend—was even better. And if an act of benevolence—such as helping the friend one was walking to meet—concluded the exercise, then it was not only healthy and enjoyable, but "sacred" as well—as "sacred" as the Victorian household itself.

Catherine Beecher entreated children, and particularly girls, to cultivate flowers and fruits in their gardens because they would be "greatly promotive of health and amusement":

It would be a most desirable improvement, if all schools for young women could be fur-

64. *Punch and Judy Show,* William H. Lippincott, American, 1896. By the end of the 19th century, the puppet shows that were eschewed as "wicked" by the pious were not only accepted once again as popular entertainment, but found a place as acceptable recreation in the families of the genteel. Long forgotten was the original violence of the Punch and Judy story, in which Punch, bludgeoned by Judy for having strangled their child, grabbed another bludgeon and beat his puppet wife to death!

nished with suitable grounds and instruments for the cultivation of fruits and flowers, and every inducement offered to engage the pupils in this pursuit. No father, who wishes to have his daughters grow up to be healthful women, can take a surer method to secure this end. Let him set apart a portion of his ground for fruits and flowers, and see that the soil is well prepared and dug over, and all the rest may be committed to the care of the children. Every man who has even half an acre could secure a small Eden around his premises.

From such an activity Catherine Beecher expected that girls would learn the noble habits of early rising, order, and neatness. In the sharing of seeds, seedlings, and final blossoms, girls could achieve refinements of the mind and learn the "feminine" ways embodied in the "passion of benevolence." She encouraged collecting seashells and geological specimens and playing games with the whole family, especially in the fresh air. Like Rousseau, she felt that, though mothers were responsible for physical health and good exercise for the entire family, fathers were still the best tutors of boys.

65. *Waterloo*, Edwin H. Blackfield, probably American, late 19th century. The isolation and frustration of the child is beautifully captured in this genre painting. His game of soldiers interrupted by the intruding world of adults, the child, about to be dispatched to the nursery, has met his "Waterloo." Presumably, the servants will set the table for two as in so many previous illustrations.

Teaching boys to use tools and encouraging them to make such useful toys as wheelbarrows, carts, and sleds, Beecher and may other 19th-century pedagogues believed, contributed to their moral and social improvement. And, if mothers could teach girls to make dolls and doll wardrobes, little girls would then learn how to cut, to fit, and finally to sew for themselves.

"Bad" amusements, the Victorian Miss Beecher assumed, had the same effect as bad exercise. Hunting and fishing for sport were evil because they instilled habits of cruelty instead of benevolence. She objected to horse racing, circus riding, theaters, games of chance, and dancing. These, of course, "aroused temptations" and stirred evil passions. The activities in themselves were not objectionable to her, but their improper regulation and the fringe excesses, which led to such vices as gambling and drunkenness, gave them their sinister character. Beecher cited dancing as an example of an

66. *Girl on a See-Saw,* John G. Brown, American, late 19th century. This painting is remarkable in its portrayal of the frailty and insecurity of childhood. Such a close-up of a child's expression would have been impossible earlier in history when there existed no notion of the child possessing an intelligence of its own. The same forces that made it possible for Freud to begin his exploration of the mind enabled artists at the turn of the century to view children more intimately.

amusement which had once been part of "sacred" life, when young and old danced together in a rural setting with fresh air all around. But no longer. In modern times, children's stomachs were first loaded with food and then the young people were overexercised in a small, close, and crowded room, becoming sweaty and creating in turn "bad air." Her idea of a healthy group amusement was a social gathering at the close of the school year in which little theatricals and a dance were held, either outside or in a large room with a broad chimney. Either way, indoors or out, they would be provided with fresh air. In addition, she preferred everyone to wear a "decent" costume and for the gathering to end by nine o'clock. Though well-intentioned, the Catherine Beechers of this world helped in part to return the Victorian child to the pent-up puritanical world of the 17th century, although there was at least some room for compromise.

But what compromise! Card-playing for children was "more safe than dangerous" if practiced under parental guidance in the home—but only because "recriminations" were as sinful as the game itself. With novel reading, she was also moderate, realizing that the parables and the allegories in the Bible were works of the imagination, too. Her recommendation regarding the reading of fiction was for parents, teachers, and

67. *Boon Companions*, James Wells Champney, American, 1879. The toys that rich men's sons played with were frequently passed down to more common folk in the pages of contemporary magazines. Full descriptions for making the "dancing doll" that is so entertaining this infant in its highchair were given in *The American Agriculturist* in 1870 and most likely appeared in other sources as well.

ministers to cull the child's character and decide for themselves whether the child's imagination would be helped or hurt by it. Phlegmatic children, she thought, could use some excitement, but imaginative children might be frightened by unrealistic literature.

In spite of all the moral platitudes and the well-intentioned arguments of 19th-century ministers, mothers, and educators, moral reformers fought a losing battle against a new and unanticipated enemy—mass production. There exists a strange contradiction between the pedagogical literature and the art of the Victorian period. On the one hand, Catherine Beecher and her distaff colleagues espoused an otherworldly atmosphere of "sacred play." On the other, contemporary paintings and prints demonstrate an abundance of toys and games and amusements very much of this world. From bicycles and building blocks to doll carriages and hoops and tops, the world of children in Victorian art is a world of commercial, mass-produced, isolating toys. Whether in the solitude of the nursery or outside on the front lawn or in the park, the 19th-century child—separated from the life of his elders—was literally surrounded by his toys—dozens of them—his loneliness assuaged only by the new materialism of childhood. Not for nothing was the Victorian era the age that virtually invented Santa Claus.

68. *The Birch Switch*, from *Children's Delight* (Boston, 1889).

4.

The Learning Child

The young child which lieth in the cradle is both wayward and full of affections; and though his body be but small, yet he hath a [wrong-doing] heart, and is altogether inclined to evil. If this sparkle be suffered to increase, it will rage over and burn down the whole house. For we are changed and become good not by birth but by education . . . .

A Godly Form of Household Government (1621)

The possibility that man could civilize himself through education, that human effort could somehow eradicate evil, is one of those dazzling rays of sunshine that occasionally break through the clouds of 17th-century Calvinism. Even those best educated among us today—members of a generation that considers schooling an inborn right and thinks of schools as indigenous to the natural landscape as flowers and trees—rarely think of the 17th-century principle that has made such complaisance possible. The assumption that the child, though containing the seeds of both good and evil, is nonetheless perfectable in human hands, is one of the major underpinnings on which the modern world rests. The perfectability of the child through education was an idea of almost stunning optimism that stands in dramatic relief to the beliefs of the Christian past. For centuries people had believed that perfection could come only as a gift to those who withdrew from the world, and not to those who worked in it. The education of the child, therefore, reflected a new hope that human participation was of some value and influence in the scheme of the universe and could affect the planetary influences on men and even overwhelm the catastrophes of famine, drought, disease, and death. Within a century this new optimistic vision was like the ever-widening ripples from a pebble tossed into a pond: educating the child to the "good life" was practical and would bring the benevolent blessings of the good life to everyone on earth.

But the "new" education of early modern times depended largely on habits formed in the Middle Ages in schools that were literal only about Scripture, scientific only about computing the date of Easter, and artistic only about that modal liturgical music called plainsong. The school was not always a formal place of study, nor was it the cultural institution that it is today or a place in which to set the child in his proper niche in life. After the collapse of the ancient city schools in the 6th century, the medieval church turned schools from centers of culture to centers of Christianity, from royal Roman training grounds to places where country boys of any age and any mentality could study to become clergymen.

Elementary education—simple instruction in reading, writing, religion, and speaking the mother tongue—was provided at home, the place where children were born or were later apprenticed, and also at choir schools or song schools where the young "scholars," as they were called, learned to recite and sing prayers, psalms, and plainsong from memory. Because there were no printed texts until the end of the 15th century, education was therefore largely oral. In the choir school, the medieval boy learned not only to sing but to read a little Latin—the living language of clerks, lawyers, and physicians—and the bare rudiments of writing. School was much as Chaucer had described it—a place for small children to sing, to read, and to learn "small grammar." Girls, unlike their opposite sex, did not go to school. But then, of course, they were believed not to possess reason.

Schools in the 15th century were usually free. Boys generally put in an eight- to ten-hour day for a year or two, four or five years of education not becoming the standard school cycle until the 18th century. Children used wooden tablet hornbooks for their ABC's, and they were provided with catechisms and sometimes an extract of Aesop's *Fables.* They had benches in their schools, but they were expected to bring all the other accoutrements of learning—writing paper, notebooks, quill pens, and knives for cutting the pens and wax candles in wintertime.

From the choir school developed the grammar school and the petty or little school, the latter remaining the simplest form of learning and the former becoming associated with the university. The grammar school concerned itself primarily with the first two of the three subjects that made up the medieval *trivium*—the so-called "trivial" studies of grammar, rhetoric, and logic—and only secondarily with the *quadrivium,* or the more practical studies of arithmetic, music, geometry, and astronomy. The medieval *trivium* was related to the literary arts and to the teaching of religion and of Latin, Greek, and Hebrew—the languages of religion. Whereas the *trivium* was first in importance and was free to all, the *quadrivium*—which contained the extra, more "use-

XI. *Henry Frederick, Prince of Wales, and Sir John Harinton,* Robert Peake, British, 1603. The education of royal males consisted more in learning the fine points of stag hunting than in perusing the texts of arts and letters. Sir John's plumed hat is removed in deference to the higher station of his companion, a motif frequently repeated in portraiture.

XII. *Picking Flowers*, artist unknown,
American, c. 1845. Robert Browning's
contemporaneous line, "God's in his
heaven—All's right with the world," is
reflected in this image of childhood
propriety. The subtle opposition of
eternal enemies—the bird and the cat—is
somehow resolved when "all the good old
orthodox flowers of stately family and
valid pretensions" bloom on a sunny day.

XIII. *Brothers*, artist unknown, American, c. 1845.
That the association of sweet, luscious fruit with
children was by no means limited to portraits of
girls is obvious in this superb evocation of
brotherly affection. The younger brother holds a
peasant cap, immensely popular in the mid-19th
century.

XIV. *Joseph and Anna Raymond,* artist unknown, American, c. 1840. Aside from the sexual distinction of their toys, a young brother and sister remain neutered in their childhood pantaloons and frocks with cowl necklines. The mug behind the little boy is inscribed "A Present for Joseph."

XV. *New England School,* Charles Frederick Bosworth, Sr., American, 1852. The one-room rural schoolhouse, in which a single schoolmarm instructed all ages and grades, was not always a model of order and deportment. The adolescent couple behind the teacher would seem to indicate that the young scholars mastered both the love of learning and of each other.

XVI. *A Ceremonial at a Young Ladies' Seminary,* artist unknown, American, c. 1810. The month of May at the Litchfield Female Academy in Connecticut was the time of music and ladylike celebration. The neoclassical garb, indigenous to the period, was revived in the later 19th century by many women's colleges and survived in collegiate Maytime pageants until well into the 20th century.

HE RETURNS NO MORE.

XVII. *He Returns No More*, Paul Schnitzler, American, 1868.
The child's involvement in the world of adult cares, frequently
treated with increasing sentimentality during the 19th century, is
here starkly portrayed in this post-Civil War painting, more than
likely copied from a contemporary print.

110

XVIII. *The Newsboy*, George Newell Bowers, American, 1889. The arrival of the working-class child at the artist's studio is a wry comment on the Gilded Age's almost grotesque fascination with so-called "street urchins." In contradistinction to the grim photographs of such reformers as Jacob Riis, many salon painters sanitized and romanticized newsboys and shoeshine boys, becoming in turn the antecedents of such artists of childhood saccharine as Walter Keane.

XIX. *Making a Train*, Seymour Joseph Guy, American, 1867. In the seclusion of her attic room where, ironically, a copy of Reynold's *Infant Samuel Praying* dangles from a nail in the wall, the rite of passage from innocence to young womanhood is enacted. Less than a generation later, a similar theme was treated unromantically in Edvard Munch's grim masterpiece, *Puberty*.

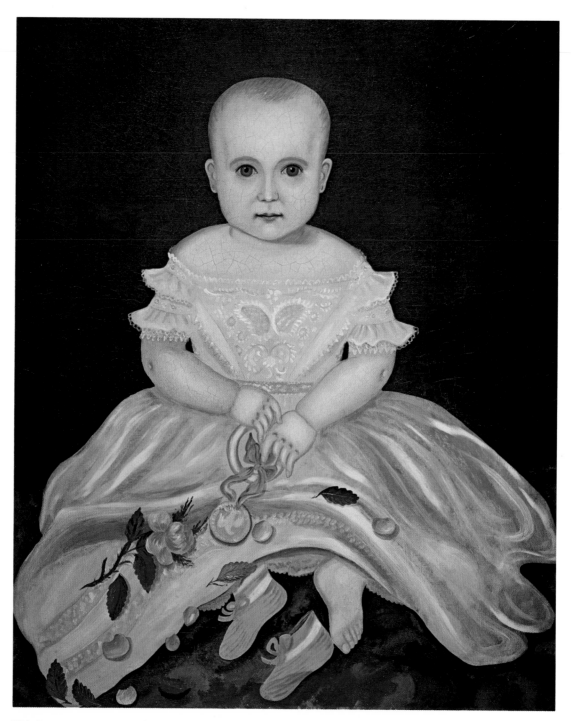

XX. *Innocence*, artist unknown, American, c. 1830. With "one shoe off and one shoe on," the baby is as much an embodiment of infantile mischief as of innocence. But the fallen rose and the medallion bearing the eagle of Resurrection suggest that the child was very likely painted from death, perhaps explaining the undeniably haunting quality of the portrait.

ful" subjects—required a payment of fees. As important as arithmetic seems today in the work of accounting, commerce, and keeping of shop or household records, it was never confused in medieval times with the real business of a school education—the classical languages. To a large extent medieval arithmetic was deemed irrelevant to the aims of a thorough education. Even so many centuries ago, a line was drawn between what was considered useful (or "mechanical" as medieval man would have called it) and what was considered "liberal" or literary.

The fine or visual arts were thought of as "mechanical" arts. Slow to develop a respectable position for their arts in the hierarchy of school curricula and in society in general, artisans and craftsmen were socially below merchants, clergymen, free-holders, farmers, and shopkeepers, the manual tasks of the artist-painter and the house-painter or of the sculptor and the stonemason remaining basically undifferentiated. Like arithmetic and the foreign languages, the visual arts—if they were taught at all—were presented in relation to trades, and their mastery was intended to put money in the pocket of the workingman-to-be. In the homes of the Protestant pious in subsequent centuries, the visual arts carried an additional stigma as they were considered ornamental, useless, and sinfully sensual.

In an age that readily accepts the "best" education as one of the perquisites of the rich and well-born, the fact that medieval schools were for everyone *but* the rich comes as a surprise. Moreover, wealthy young men wanted no part of the medieval curriculum. The idea of acquiring "cultivation" in the classroom would have been a notion quite foreign to them. The church, the law, and the world of medicine, it must be remembered, provided *occupational* advancement for poor boys and not *background* for the elite. The gentry despised learning, in fact, and thought that a formal education was in every way a social handicap. In every practical sense they hardly needed to rise above their illiteracy. Nobles and gentlemen did not *need* Latin, reading, or writing, because in their station they could hire clerical scribes to keep their records for them and because the larger part of their daily business was conducted orally. Even in the early 16th century, the children of very few noblemen attended either the petty or grammar schools or the universities. These were left to the children of the meaner sorts who needed the technical skills of reading and writing to find a workingman's place in the world. The sons of the rich and titled were educated at home, on the playing field, in the gymnasium, at the dance, and, more often than not, abroad. These young noblemen received a minimally literate education in the great house or in the monasteries where they served as pages, oblates, or clerks. By the 17th century when England, unlike other European countries, encouraged gentlemen to keep in close proximity to the merchant class, noble and genteel sons were sometimes apprenticed to merchants as a way of familiarizing them with the foreign languages of trade so that they might one day control commerce. The original purpose for schooling the sons of the genteel and for sending them out to service, however, was to prepare them for the responsibility of maintaining property, government, and the larger number of people always in their charge rather than to prepare them for success in the wage-earning world.

Girls, being considered inferior in temperament and condition and different in divine purpose, received an education a world apart from boys. Not admitted to 15th-century choir schools nor to 16th-century grammar schools, they learned their reading, writing, and religion either at the home in which they were born or worked, or in the petty schools that eventually developed into the dame and academy schools of the 18th and 19th centuries. Although the lot of the distaff student remained for centuries restrictive at best, at least one Renaissance thinker enunciated a somewhat modern view of female education. Baldassare Castiglione, author of *The Courtier* (translated, 1561), the foremost book of etiquette of its day, thought girls should receive training in at least foreign languages and in music. Moreover, he recommended that they be able to draw and paint, be active in sports and pastimes, and know how to

69. *Medieval Petty School*, from *Rudimenta Grammaticae* (Venice, 1492). The older scholars, most likely learning their Latin, assemble around the master. The younger boys, with wooden hornbooks, sit on benches close to the ground which they share with an animal. The scholars are dressed identically in robes and are unusual for the time only because most possess books. One imagines that they paid dearly if the rule of silence was disobeyed.

dance well. His advice, which dared to revive the classical connection between music and education in the raising of girls, had its greatest impact in the late 18th century, when no properly educated young woman of class was unable to sing or play at the pianoforte. A much debated pedagogical issue that survived well into the Victorian era, the encouragement of music and dance in the life of girls was often interpreted by the pious as a signal of the devil at work.

Music, taught at home in genteel households throughout the medieval and modern periods, was by the 18th century an "accomplishment," a "refinement," an "ornamental" study that was never to be taken seriously by girls or practiced professionally. The "heavenly" stringed instruments of harpsichord and guitar were considered soothing and appropriate for genteel girls. But more pious families—as if remembering the seduction symbolized by the bagpipes of medieval monks in the illuminations of the past—condemned music for girls, especially wind music, on the grounds that it excited the passions, weakened the body, and tempted the already "quivering" female

70. *Portrait of a Gentleman and His Son after the Hunt*, Francis Wheatley, British, 1779. A young gentleman learned his lessons not only in school, but from his father in the field. The education of a young aristocrat was perhaps never better described than by Byron in *Don Juan:* "He learned the arts of riding, fencing, gunnery, And how to scale a fortress—or a nunnery." (*See* plate XI).

soul to turn more quickly toward evil. Consequently, from about the time that Juan Luis Vives wrote about the education of females in the 16th century to the time that Catherine Beecher was the reigning expert on American family life in the 19th, the "lascivious" practice of dancing was associated with "wenches" and not with honest or "holy" women.

Among the many characteristics of medieval schools, one problem in particular was to give reformers great trouble: gradelessness. The division of students into levels or grades was unknown in the distant past and medieval educators showed no interest in distinguishing between ages just as they showed no interest in distinguishing between the tender habits of children and what later moralists would have called the "polluting sins of youth." Boys too old to remain in school, but not wanted on the streets because they were without employment, were thrown in with very young boys just entering school. Schoolmasters and parents were either inured to the sexual play bred by the

71. *Portrait of a Boy,* Matthew Pratt, American, 18th century. With the visible signs of his learning clearly evident, this handsome aristocratic young man holds a Greek text. By the end of the 18th century, the quest for a knowledge of classical languages had so become the hallmark of the sons of the genteel that it became the basis of a legend: A student, attacked by a wild boar (so the story goes), threw a volume of Aristotle into his snapping jaws, exclaiming "Graecum est" (This is Greek), and thereby choked the beast to death.

mixing of all ages of boys in one group or were simply unconcerned. Far from the fears that tormented Victorian boys about the "insanity" that followed masturbation, the medieval temperament more readily accepted Fallopius's view that masturbation was good since it enlarged the penis. Whatever, the ungradedness of the medieval school went hand in hand with its undefined hours in the school day and the undefined ages of its students, making disorder in the medieval school an acceptable educational phenomenon.

Understandably, anything even resembling regular school attendance was made impossible by the medieval practice of childhood service and apprenticeship, and attendance was cyclical, as well, because of the demands on students to work during the harvest and planting seasons. Formal education in the Middle Ages was therefore complicated by the demands of a simple agricultural society, demands made of course on other societies and on other periods of time as well. Consequently, in the America of

72. *Schoolroom*, from *The Youth's Guide* by Mordecai Stewart (Baltimore, 1820). In this early 19th-century American classroom, the sexes are clearly segregated. The boys, instructed by a male, study such "mechanical" subjects as geometry, geography, and astronomy, while the girls take instruction in needlework from a schoolmistress.

1800 as in the Europe of 1400, the primitive quality of life, the dependence on the whims of nature and of the soil, and the necessity of protecting the society as a whole made the education of the young incidental to these more pressing matters.

Similarly, just as medieval students had been grouped together in ages from eight to twenty-five years, American students were grouped in ages from four to twenty-three in local schools and from eight to twenty-five in academies. Throughout the 19th century this group form of teaching still prevailed in the common elementary schools of America, with up to the astonishing number of 1,000 assembling in one large room, although the number was usually very much smaller. (Just how primitive were conditions in these one-room schoolhouses may be seen in 19th-century recipes for homemade children's ink: salt was to be added to prevent mold in hot weather, and brandy was to be added as a sure antifreeze.) Whether large groups of children remained ungraded because schools have always been easy to use as detention centers and their masters as surrogate police officers, and whether, in fact, the problem was only accentuated in later years by the declining practices of childhood service and apprenticeship which had formerly kept children busy and trained them for work, remain unanswerable questions. But to the moralists of the 17th century, the mixing of children with young adults, in part responsible for disorder in the schools, was a dangerous condition, the work of the devil meant to challenge their faith. It would follow logically that when Sunday schools were eventually developed, they were very carefully agegraded.

By the 17th century in England, Protestant reformers, largely middle class, took over the schools. Religion continued to dominate the school curriculum under Pro-

73. *Scenes from a Seminary for Young Ladies* (detail), artist unknown, American, 1810-20. A few years before an anonymous schoolgirl recorded this remarkable scene, Enos Hitchcock, a progressive thinker for his time, recommended the study of geography for girls: "How profitably might young females spend their time in reading history, biography, travels, voyages.... To these I would add geography, both as an agreeable study, and as *requisite* to the reading of the others."

testant control, but clergymen replaced the old methods of oral study with reading texts and in particular with readings from the Bible and kindred pious books. As the new printing trade grew, more and more religious texts appeared on the market to feed the spiritual appetites of the Age of Faith. Schoolmasters themselves became more literate and also more knowledgeable about Scripture than had been medieval teachers, and the laity—the parents themselves—learned to read. Noble families, pressured by the competition of the new reading middle class and sensing that their political positions would no longer be easy to inherit, sent their sons to the grammar schools to learn how to read and to master Latin. Following attendance in the grammar schools, they matriculated in the universities and, for law, the Inns of Court. Suddenly it became fashionable for the upper-class boy to receive what was then called a "book education."

In the 16th century Sir William Cecil, Lord Burghley, had been among the first to set the style of educating aristocratic boys. For the twelve-year-old Edward, Earl of Ox-

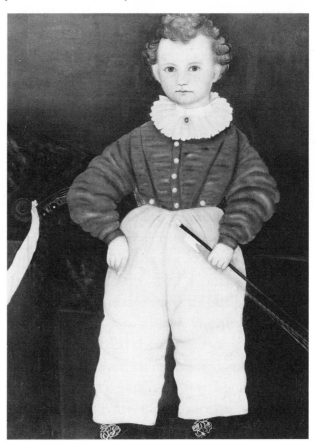

74. *Young Boy with a Violin*, artist unknown, American, 19th century. The playing of musical instruments, though frowned on by the evangelical, was almost always a sign of accomplishment among the genteel. The upper classes would most certainly have agreed with Dr. Johnson that music "is the only sensual pleasure without vice."

ford, who like his peers was to be educated in field hunting, hawking, and practicing with the longbow, he laid down a course of study that included such very new and liberal subjects as French, composition, and drawing, in addition to the usual Latin and prayers. The young earl was requested to study all his subjects before dinner at noon and to repeat the morning studies in the afternoon. To this routine Burghley added another new subject, cosmography, that in combining geography and physics was believed to encourage among aristocratic boys the equally new trading spirit of the 16th century. After supper young Oxford repeated the whole series once more.

Lord Burghley's success with Oxford and with the sons of other noblemen led directly to the fashion of a "bookish education" for young aristocrats. And with other social classes reaching out as well for a school education, the consequence was the establishment in the 17th century of new schools for separate social classes—for the poor, for artisans, for farmers, for merchants, and for the genteel. The rationale for the separate education of the classes was perhaps best stated a century later by James Nelson in *An Essay on the Government of Children* (1768):

> Let me ask a natural Question: What is it all Mankind aim at in the Education of their Children? certainly to give them such a Degree of Knowledge as will qualify them to fill some certain Post, some certain Station in Life: in short, to fit them for an Employment suited to their Condition, such as will make them happy in themselves, and useful to Society.

Working boys could attend trade schools, and, if they were from liberal merchant families, they had the advantages of such new academies as were designed to train youths in experimental science, modern languages, dancing, vaulting, music, and, as in the past, hunting or "riding the great horse." Subjects were taught in English and the use of textbooks was encouraged. Virtuosos, usually the eldest sons in families who stood to inherit family property, could also attend these same "Italianated" academies or take the Grand Tour. Hardly requiring an education for the purpose of finding work, they studied to make themselves fit for conversation in polite society, and with them was born the art of learning for its own sake.

The difference in attitude between the new scholars—the gentleman and the pious man—was epitomized in the battle over the "liberal" or "trivial" arts. Reforming Protestants, joined by such gentlemen as Lord Burghley, discredited the liberal Italianate academies and the education derived from travel abroad on the Grand Tour by claiming that education was the business of God alone and that foreign influences menaced no less than a man's body, a man's soul, the English nation, and the Protestant point of view. Such writers as Roger Ascham in the 16th century, Edward Waterhouse a hundred years later, and American moralists for centuries to come excoriated as "injurious" for young scholars the liberal arts of "other" nations. "The less youth knows of the levity, liberty, shifts, profaneness, atheism, subtlety, and lubricity of other nations," wrote Waterhouse, "the more are they probable to be solid, circumspect, plain, devout, pious, modest."

What can be called "progress" in education began, then, in the 17th century and implied the separation of ages and classes, the improvement in literacy, and the restriction of reading materials to include only the moral and self-correcting literature and the *quadrivium* or the "mechanical" arts. The general trend toward producing "useful" children who were prepared for eternity was to blossom in the new schools of America and in a new subject that was to serve as a replacement for the Grand Tour—geography.

When teaching geography, the master emphasized the practical—the language, commerce, manufacture, government, and military strength of a country—and the

75. *Young Woman at a Piano,* artist unknown, American, 19th century. Music was an important element in the education of an accomplished young woman. One authority on childhood "management," James Nelson, wrote that "a young lady of class should learn Music; it gives her a sprightly pleasing Air; it is a fine Relaxation from more serious Employments [and] greatly contributes to keep up a Chearfulness thro' the whole Family...."

spiritual—the map of God's earthly world and the "geographic" routes of the traveling patriarchs, prophets, evangelists, apostles, and even of Christ himself. Even Sir Walter Raleigh's *History of the World* (1614), popular on both sides of the Atlantic and a geography of sorts, included fifteen sections on the position of Paradise and a map to show its location. The advertisement within a typical book used by early 19th-century children—Nathaniel Dwight's *A Short But Comprehensive System of the Geography of the World* (1806)—clearly states the broad purpose of the subject:

> Geography opens to our view much of the wisdom and goodness of the creator, in making various and bountiful provision for his creatures, in appointing them their residence in different parts of the globe, and suiting their capacities to their respective circumstances. It teaches us that mankind are one great family, though different in their complexions, situations and habits. It promotes social intercourse and mutual happiness.

76. *The Botanists*, artist unknown, American, c. 1835. In reviewing *A Child's First Book of Botany* (1871) by a Miss Youmans, one distaff coummentator wrote that "Botany is one of the best things possible for cultivating the awakening faculties of a child, if taught very gradually and always as a pleasure to the child, never as a task, or when its heart is set on something else."

Two problems were to confront both the pious educators and those gentlemen who favored the liberal arts—the situation of the poor who were being pushed out of the educational circle and the challenge of Rousseau's doctrine of divine childhood innocence. Poor children, who had been absorbed by the schools in medieval days, were unable to find a place in the early modern educational institutions that had been geared to the orderliness advocated by the influential writings of John Locke. The key for this important writer on "the good life" was in good habits signalled by regularity in reading, work, bodily relief, sleep, and exercise. Consequently, the school year was eventually divided into four quarters with three vacations of twelve to twenty-one days each, and the length of one's schooling was normalized to six or sometimes seven years. With the flexibility of medieval schools a thing of the past, the irregular schedules of poor children in service or apprenticeship could no longer be accommodated. Therefore, by the end of the 17th century and into the 18th, the numbers of poor children in attendance dwindled in the grammar schools on both sides of the Atlantic.

77. Alfred Openshaw, Born July 1846, R. Hunt, British, c. 1849. Such writers as Catherine Beecher saw in ducks, chickens, and other barnyard animals a natural way to stimulate benevolence within the child. Such animals, these writers reasoned, did not cry out in hunger like the cat, but waited dependently for human help.

With problems on the street increasing as idle children turned more and more to petty crime to stay alive, a new variation on the grammar school began in 1699 as charity schools opened their doors for the first time. Such institutions as the Burlington School for girls in London taught arithmetic, writing, and "cast accounts one afternoon in a Week," but these charity schools were, however, little more than workhouses producing textile and domestic needlework pieces.

By the 18th century a good number of men were entirely opposed to any sort of education for the poor. Bernard de Mandeville, in his famous *Fable of the Bees* (1714), proposed that knowledge would only enlarge poor children's desires beyond fulfillment and make boys unfit as grown-ups for "downright Labour." But in the 1790s in America, Noah Webster, more sympathetic to the virtues of all men and to the hearts of children, complained that Americans, with the full support of the law in several states, educated only people of property while neglecting provisions for people of poorer rank. His concern foreshadowed by many years the establishment of a uniquely American common school movement.

The Sunday school movement of the late 18th century—a formal union of education and morality—produced the best charity schools in England and America. Financed by private contributions largely from the middle classes, Sunday schools were free, were open to girls, and existed to serve very poor children in their religious, moral, and practical needs. Held on the Sabbath, these charity schools allowed poor children to work during the week without being completely denied a rudimentary education—and also kept the streets free and peaceful on the Lord's day. But even in the

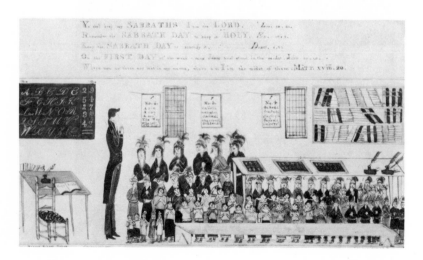

78. *Seneca Mission Schoolhouse*, Dennis Cusick, American, c. 1827. In this rare scene of an Indian mission school, the pupils, wearing headdresses and arranged by age, are being instructed in the proper way to observe the Christian Sabbath. On the wall hang reading charts in English and (phonetically) in the Senecan language. The blackboard reveals instruction in penmanship and in arithmetic. A bible is open on the master's desk. A primary purpose of such schools was to train Indians to become missionaries to their own people.

Sunday schools, class distinctions were never entirely forgotten. As one minister sermonized in 1785:

> The children should be taught to read, & be instructed in the plain duties of the Christian Religion with a particular view to their future character as labourers and servants.

The first free schools for poor children in America were those devised in 1787 by Benjamin Rush of Philadelphia. These were based on the success of church-related schools established by the Society of Friends in England and in Pennsylvania. Inspired by the Quaker Anthony Benezet and his principles of free education for all, Rush recommended not only the study of English, and of German for those who requested it, but of needlework, knitting, and spinning for girls. "Above all," Rush wrote,

> let both sexes be carefully instructed in the principles and obligations of the Christian religion. This is the most essential part of education—this will make them dutiful children, teachable scholars, and, afterwards, good apprentices, good husbands, good wives, honest mechanics, industrious farmers, peaceable sailors, and, in everything that relates to this country, good citizens.

79. *Fifteen Girls and Schoolmarm*, artist unknown, American, late 19th century. Although the girls clearly outnumber their schoolmarm, the teacher nonetheless looms large in this fascinating picture. As public education as well as education for females became the norm by the end of the century, teachers became the new priests, preparing their little "parishioners" for a new secular salvation. This charming construction of watercolor cut-outs pasted on posterboard evokes the new importance of the teacher: "Magnify your office, teacher!/ Higher than the kings of earth;—/ Are you not the prophet preacher,/ To the future giving birth?"

The education of blacks, Indians, and other minorities in the early years of the republic was, if anything, even less comprehensive than that offered poor whites. In the American South many schoolmasters and ministers educated slaves to the reading of the Bible, simple writing, and memorization of their catechisms. Education for Indian children was provided by the Society for the Propagation of the Gospel, the Anglican missionary movement, the Moravian missionaries, by such men as John Eliot, David Brainerd, and Eleazar Wheelock in New England, and the Catholic padres in the Southwest. Missionaries provided the best source of minority education in America, although even among them the old fear remained that with education might come rebellion.

In the midst of the educational turmoil over the respective virtues or vices of little schools, grammar schools, private schools, charity schools, and missionary schools, the other important condition to challenge and change the education of the pious and the genteel alike was the belief in the divinity of youth which arose in the person of Jean Jacques Rousseau. Optimistic, but somewhat impractical and occasionally inconsis-

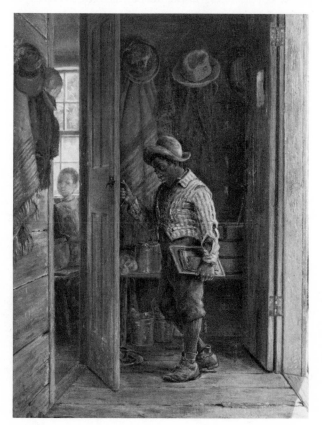

80. *Tardy*, E. L. Henry, American, late 19th century. Unlike the gross caricatures of black children that were rampant in America after 1880 or so, this painting, though no less sentimental than other late 19th-century art, is at least sympathetic. Note that the one-room schoolhouse attended by blacks is as primitive and bleak as those attended by white rural children. Contemporary sources indicate that such schools were founded through the efforts of black parents.

tent, he concluded in 1762 that God's human child was altogether and absolutely innocent, perfect, and not to be tampered with by man, traditional education, reformed education, or any education until he was twelve years of age. He fathered respect for the child, freedom for the child, and a life of natural but hard work for the child.

Rousseau, sanctifying the rule of nature, upset the 17th-century order of reformed educators and brought back some of the flexibility of the 15th-century school. Although his theories did not revive the communality of medieval life—his ideal child was always to be tutored alone—they did reflect a resistance to intellectual life for children—no reading or moralizing, for example—and a resistance to play for its own sake. Pleasure, responsibility, and freedom consisted for him in learning to work and to make the things that one wanted. To desire in turn what one had made closed the gaps between a child's ability, his accessions, and his appetite. Rousseau would have exercised the healthy child's body and rested the healthy child's mind. At twelve—the age of loving commitment—the French philosopher would have children read *Robinson Crusoe* to encourage independence and the classical writers to bring them closer to nature and to the beauties of Greek and Roman culture.

When it came to the education of girls, Rousseau was a bit more hierarchical and medieval in tone. Higher studies for girls were unnecessary and in fact useless, he believed, since girls were after all observant but not reasonable, witty but not bright, and bound by tradition to provide pleasure and comfort to those around them. Health, grace, and charm were to be products of a female education that included the dance, song, the art of speaking, the knowledge of plants and animals, and the domestic

81. *The Country School*, Winslow Homer, American, 1871. Not everyone appreciated the blessings of universal education. Mark Twain, for example, wrote that "Soap and education are not as sudden as a massacre, but they are more deadly in the long run." Common schools in America were, in fact, in various states of decay. They were without privies, too small, destitute of all kinds of apparatus, and they had only benches without backs and rarely blackboards.

talents of sewing and lacemaking. Still possessing the defects of original sin, girls were to Rousseau very much like the young wild devils at medieval fairs—innately fickle, unpredictable, vain, and sensual, needing the restraints of religion much more than did boys.

Despite the fact that a good number of debatable nuances within Rousseau's complex educational theories were rejected by many Americans as elitist and ultimately idle, he and his fictitious boy-child Émile nonetheless ushered in the great and innocent age of the child. Rousseau loosened the intrusive hold adults maintained on childhood and in addition inspired doctors from Germany, England, and America to reconstruct health standards based on his simplistic views of the outdoors and of dress. He reprimanded parents for subjecting children to formal learning before the age of five, and teachers for training children by rote instead of by original reflection.

By opening the doors to spontaneous learning, to relatively painless education, and by inspiring the writing of books with such liberal titles as the mid-19th-century *My Play Is Study*, Rousseau unintentionally encouraged a host of romantic writers to use each enjoyable, natural, and delightful event in daily life as a way of depicting grim moral points. Tying down every happy moment to deep ethical evaluations of life, and sometimes to the Christian "beauty" of youthful death, was not exactly what Rousseau had in mind when he recommended "experiencing" wisdom. But the spiritual morality that we perhaps unfairly call "Victorian" was surely one result of his writing.

The sentimental writers of England and America who followed him—Lord Kames, Mrs. Trimmer, Hannah More, Mary Wollstonecraft, Anna L. Barbauld, Richard and Maria Edgeworth, John Aiken, Thomas Day, Enos Hitchcock—and who attended to the heart instead of the head, shifted the educational center once more toward the home and the very small private school. Helped by the evangelical enthusiasm of George Whitefield, John Wesley, and Horace Bushnell, parents began to see home education as an intellectual and moral practicality. Moderate, pious, and genteel families moved conservatively toward the home tutor and the small church school, reinforced by Rousseau's preference for a natural and private education and by the general trend in living toward privacy, domesticity, individualism, and elitism. In England and in the American South, many small private schools sprang up, resembling early Quaker schools for the indigent and even earlier medieval schools, but offering a curriculum that was more commercial and social than classical and linguistic. Writing, arithmetic, English, navigation, foreign languages, dancing, music, drawing, fencing, and needlework were taught, the last five subjects required additional fees.

Anna Barbauld, Mary Wollstonecraft, Hannah More, Sarah Pierce, and Susanna Rowson are among the more notable examples of female writer-teachers who ran these home-like schools for children in the 19th century. They made extensive and manipulative use of Rousseau's theory of education by natural experience, inventing such animal creatures as Maria Edgeworth's "little dog Trusty" or Edward Kendall's "little crested wren" to personify heroes, while fictitious human children exemplified the cruel attributes of villains stealing eggs, breaking nests, and caging birds. Then, like one of Mrs. Barbauld's storybook boys who was so bad that he tortured and refused to feed a hungry bird and was in turn himself eaten by a wild bear, children could learn through shame and fear the morals and manners of "good" little ones.

Perhaps in Thomas Day's famous book *The History of Little Jack* (1788) can be glimpsed the true value of every child in the eyes of Jean Jacques Rousseau. Day, when responding to another writer's objection to the unreality of a nanny goat playing mother and wet nurse to a human child in the story, simply declared:

> It is of very little consequence how a man comes into the world, provided he behaves well and discharges his duty when he is in it.

Stuart Little, E. B. White's remarkable 20th-century mouse born of human parents, would have agreed.

82. *Country School*, E. L. Henry, American, late 19th century. The American one-room schoolhouse may have been "a ragged beggar sleeping," as the poet Whittier described it, but its omnipresence was a reminder of the triumph of the common school movement by the end of the century. As Robert G. Ingersoll wrote in 1886, "the most significant fact in this world today is that in nearly every village under the American flag, the schoolhouse is larger than the church."

83. *Shoeshine Boy*, Karl Witkowski, American, late 19th century.

5.

The Working Child

The golf links lie so near the mill
That almost every day
The laboring children can look out
And see the men at play.
Sarah N. Cleghorn (1915)

Work has always been a characteristic feature of the adult world. With little distinction having been placed between the child and the adult or the child and the servant in medieval days, children were early pressed into adult family service. Work was not looked upon as a degrading activity, and compared with toil in the field, domestic work could even be considered refined. As we shall see in the pages that follow, work meant getting a chance for an education; work meant being able to leave freely one's family and to join other working members in new households every few years; work meant acquiring the skills to become independent. It meant subservience to the master of the house; it meant keeping off the streets; and it meant doing God's will. The medieval child maintained his membership in a family as much by working in it as by being born into it.

The words *master* and *servant*, *binding out* and *putting out* were not offensive to the ears of the 15th-, 16th-, or 17th-century citizenry. The term *master*, in fact, suggested only positive virtues and aims—vocational training, education, good habits, and personal and political security for every member of the household. If the master also seemed to represent discipline and brutality, he shared these attributes with parents, teachers, and government officials with whom he also shared the power to govern society.

Nearly everyone was a servant at one time or another from the medieval period through the 18th century. Next to prayer, work was considered the most important influence in the bringing up of children and was the only guarantee a child had of receiving an education. There were three general types of work available to children—domestic service in the home or in the monastery, field service, and apprenticeship in shops at home. All three rested on a familial relationship between master and child, and this meant that most medieval children over seven lived the greater part of their childhoods in the home of strangers. But they were treated legally and affectionately as members of the family—that is, they were loved as well as they were beaten.

Being "put out" or sent away to work was a condition even aristocratic children understood. The children of noblemen and gentlemen served in great households as pages and ladies-in-waiting, and a few genteel boys apprenticed with the better merchants. The ability to find service and to procure a master who would train as well as house, clothe, feed, and even educate was what the parents of most children and even the children themselves sought. And from work came the appreciation of such adult skills as housewifery, husbandry, and craftsmanship; and, with luck, a degree of personal civilization and good manners.

Although the custom of medieval apprenticeship answered obvious needs—new or improved skills to be learned, relief for the family with too many children, or salvation from poverty—still, the practice, much like that of wet-nursing, continued without good reason into the 18th century, both in Europe and in the New World and in households that by that late date already possessed all the advantages for which children had been originally put out. It is tempting to speculate that sending children away may have relieved the conflicting emotions of affectionate parents for children and parental fears of being close to them in their budding sexual years, and that this unconscious relief might have been ultimately more satisfying than the purpose for which apprenticeship had been consciously designed. Apprenticeship apparently precipitated a bit early in the child's life what parents and children have always known must come—the leave-taking much later identified by Freud as separation anxiety.

Service in the centuries that followed the Middle Ages took its place beside formal schooling, a movement which was building momentum as literacy became more valuable to the prosperous and to the pious. But, as the interest in educating children grew in intensity in the modern era, and service, adulthood, and the time of separation were pushed further and further ahead, family habits of work and responsibility were lost to the child, and the key to his freedom was placed on the shelf for another day.

The historian Peter Laslett has referred to the communal working world of the Middle Ages as "the world we have lost." He admits that it was not a "paradise or golden age of equality, tolerance, or loving kindness." It was, in fact, a world exploitative of children, at times as evil and as manipulative in the home as the world of the 19th century was known to be in the manufactory. The difference between worlds, however, lay in the communality of work, in the day's effort shared by everyone, and in the acceptance of its being built into the family system. Work was the common education in life; work was the instrument that allowed children, and everyone, to survive. Work was not a glorious state, but one that had some liberating advantages.

Success—a word associated in the 17th century with divine benevolence and the spiritual status quo and in the 20th century with personal progress and with change—did not exist for medieval families who were ordained from birth to their positions in society. Because they worked for the community, they did not measure personal success nor expect to work for change. But labor in the home for the group called "family" supplied not only a basis for survival, but an adequate and permanent source of an individual's recognition. It is perhaps this source for the confirmation of self to which Peter Laslett refers when he writes of the world which we, indeed, seem to have lost.

84. *Industry & Sloth*, from *Picture Lessons, Illustrating Moral Truth* (Philadelphia, c. 1850). The Protestant work ethic is graphically illustrated in this 19th-century picture and its caption: "What a sight! The sluggard streched out in his bed with the bright light shining upon him and his mother and sister at work as busy as bees. Let him lose his breakfast two or three times and he will learn better ways."

It is astonishing to realize in this age of emphasis on vacations, play, and amusement for the young that once no one wanted to be free from work. The most difficult problem in medieval and early modern times was the lack of enough employing families to go around. Practically no one was too young to work. Infant-children were working at three in the fields, tending cattle, gathering firewood, scaring away birds, and singling turnips—working the same hours at home as were demanded of them centuries later in the factory. Very little had changed for young English chidren of laboring parents by 1697 when John Locke, the ideological father of early education, recommended that a working school be set up in every parish so that any child over three could begin to learn how to earn money for his own subsistance. In the early 18th century, children of three and four years were employed to handle lace bobbins and sort straw for rugs, dolls, and baskets. At five they were working a full day in the lace schools and were also employed plaiting the straw. At six they were earning a standard wage at such tasks.

The trade schools of the 17th century, designed as educational facilities, were usually no more than workshops for the poor, taxing the children as vigorously as many parents and masters had taxed them at home. With the development of strong class distinctions in the modern era, and new rules and regulations in the schools, poor children, who in medieval times had shared the problems of the school day and the working day with every other child, were cut off from the educational community. Signifi-

85. *Apple Gatherers*, artist unknown, American, 19th century. The virtue of work out-of-doors, recommended by Rousseau for his ideal student Emile, was endorsed by many, including Henry David Thoreau who wrote in his journal the following: "Good for the body is the work of the body, good for the soul the work of the soul, and good for either the work of the other."

cantly, when the majority of children were finally sent off to school and poor children alone were held back, the ones to complain were not the parents, but early benevolent societies and humanistic writers uttering a few small cries of protest.

What were some of the usual tasks offered to children of the late medieval and early modern period? Both boys and girls could serve in many capacities equally well. By ten they were often employed to bake bread, brew beer, catch fish, butcher animals, and roast meat. But only boys could apprentice with craftsmen. Most tradesmen took them at twelve, although some took them as young as seven. Child labor changed very little in the rural countryside into the 19th century. Fairs, especially at May Day in market towns, were still the places where men found young children for hire on the farm. Young boys entered what was referred to in England as a "bullring," and by some clergymen as a slave market. From it farmers chose servants, the bullring being the only way, they claimed, to see the children before hiring them. Jobs were rarely expected to be permanent. After each "pag-rag" day, or payday to use the modern term, they collected their wages and left their masters for a visit home and another job. The public gang was a group of children often hired full time by a ganger or gangmaster who subcontracted child laborers to different farmers. The gangmaster oversaw the children and kept them at their work. The farmer often made if compulsory for children to work on the Sabbath day, refusing to hire them for the other six unless they worked on the seventh.

At the age of twelve, girls had new options—dressmaking, field or dairy work, or the care of aged parents. And then, of course, there was domestic service, always considered a more refined employment for girls than field work because young females could best respond to their "submissive" natures by the hearth. Like their education, very little changed for girls in their workaday world until the 19th century. To grow into women of "understanding and goodness," they were expected to serve in ways that would continue to make them feel modest, protected, and feminine. In later centuries when poor girls and farm girls left home for work in the factories, they were actually thought to have given up the dictates of a female nature.

The apprenticeship system in England and America was essentially a medieval form of child labor wrenched from its original communal context. Without this sense of communal responsibility, however, laws were needed to enforce the system. The Elizabethan Statute of Artificers, first instituted in 1563, controlled the apprenticeship contract and made seven years a compulsory time for child and master to share education in the trade. The seven-year terms for craft instruction protected young workers from the competition of outsiders who had not fulfilled this requirement, while assuring the public of well-trained workmen and acceptable goods. The statute, an official government order, was enforced in England by the trade guilds. In America, with no guilds to serve as watchdogs, it was sometimes ignored by such craftsmen as the young Benjamin Franklin.

Children were not paid for their services under apprenticeship contracts, but they were usually the recipients of "meat, drink, clothes, washing, and lodging." The promises of a good education in the chosen trade and of literacy were not always fulfilled. Where Americans were sometimes short of the required years for apprenticeship, they were often strong on enforcing the requirements for education. In Massachusetts, Connecticut, and New York, educational requirements were established in the 17th century, requiring apprentices to receive instruction "in matters of Religion and the Laws of the country...and in some honest and Lawful Calling." Any master in

86. *Christmas Presents Made Here*, artist unknown, British or American, c. 1875. Although the ability of a boy to use woodworking tools was a virtue long praised, the fad for fretwork which lasted for several decades of the late 19th century enabled virtually any schoolboy to transform thin wood into openwork brackets, picture frames, towel racks, and small ornaments. Here a boy is busily engaged in producing Christmas gifts for the entire family.

Massachusetts who was illiterate and could not himself instruct his apprentices was obliged to send them to school. In New York and Philadelphia, night schools were established for apprentices so that masters who needed help could fulfill their responsibilities.

Work meant not only a good education and independence for the child, but protection for the society at large. A child out of work—especially a boy child and, even more frightening, a *poor* boy child—threatened the peace of the streets. And it was commonly believed that children of artisan and laboring families without work would be doomed to a future of vagrancy and jail.

Children loose on the streets were a social problem no less important in the time of Henry VIII and Edward VI than in the time of Queen Victoria and Abraham Lincoln or

87. *An Eligible Opportunity,* artist unknown, British [reprinted in *Harper's Magazine* (March, 1853)]. Abuses in the apprenticeship system had always existed, but in the 19th century writers and artists were freer to speak out in outrage. The result was satire such as this or such poems as Elizabeth Barrett Browning's *The Cry of the Children:* "The child's sob in the silence curses deeper/ Than the strong man in his wrath."

in our own. By formal acts first passed in England at the end of the 16th century, society was "protected" from children who were not in training. Any child not of the gentlemanly class (that is, of parents who owned at least some land and goods and cattle) could be put out by town officials in any sort of apprenticeship position that could be found. Anyone under the age of twenty-one refusing this apprenticeship could be imprisoned.

On the other hand, the child himself was protected from men who wanted to be masters but who were financially unable to support apprentices. A master was obliged in turn to prove that he, too, was economically responsible, that he, too, owned a reasonable amount of land. English landowners could engage any apprentice between the ages of ten and eighteen and keep him until he was twenty or twenty-four. Additionally, any child who was put out by his own parents was also screened according to property requirements. If his parents could not prove their ownership of land, the master merchant or tradesman was not usually required to take on the boy as an apprentice. The amount of land and goods owned by parents frequently determined the acceptance of boys as apprentices to such specialized craftsmen as goldsmiths, ironmongers, embroiderers, and woolen-cloth weavers.

These economic restrictions effectively froze the easy social mobility of children by placing each child in whatever craft the trade guild preferred for him, a decision based on family wealth. In the case of English fine woolen-cloth weavers, these restrictions closed off apprenticeships to the children of three-quarters of the rural population. The lower crafts of smith, wheelwright, ploughwright, shingler, carpenter, tilemaker, linemaker, and plain-woolen weavers of household cloth, however, welcomed children from families without any land. The subtle distinctions of status in the trades grew with other social differences in the early modern era of reform.

In colonial America, where a ready supply of land was short, men were not held tightly to the Statute of Artificers. Children, more often than not, completed four of the seven allotted learning years, their parents not always fulfilling the required property qualifications. In the colonies that raised tobacco crops, the apprentices were mostly poor or vagrant children who were forced to work, and their term was usually stretched to a period longer than four years.

In the manner in which the upper class expected its status to be visible in the clothing it wore, the guilds required its young apprentices to be distinguished from their masters by dressing as apprentices. As a result, young boys were identified by their dress as working adults rather than by their age as children. The apprentice, as early as 1595 and as late as 1890, wore a cap. He was required to dress "not obstinately"—that is, plainly and not extravagantly—and to keep from having long hair. To violate the accepted norm of dress was to court imprisonment. Even if apprentices from wealthier families overdressed for their laboring positions, they forfeited work time already served and were publicly whipped for their social indiscretion. Their masters were also liable for the fines levied if they had permitted improper clothing to be worn by their charges.

Although the typical child apprentice wore a smock, boots, and a cap—a costume later fashionably imitated by the democratic elite—it was the cap that symbolized his hope in the future, the cap that showed his pride in the present, the cap that signalled servitude, and the cap that he kept when he earned his freedom. Among the English

88. *Happy Tim*, from *Children's Delight* (Boston, 1889). No such chimney sweep as "Happy Tim" ever existed, but the Victorians, firmly believing in the work ethic, so extolled the virtues of labor that such happy child laborers were created in children's books as moral emblems for impressionable youngsters. The photographs of Lewis W. Hine and Jacob Riis put an end eventually to such manipulative fantasies as "Happy Tim."

writers of 17th-century books for apprentices was one who first saw in clothing a symbol of working for change:

> If you disdaine not to weare a Prentices Cap, you may live to see the Cap of Maintenance, worn before you as the Cities Praetor. Put on those clothes of a servant cheerfully, which your Master shall bestow upon you, and this City which is now your Nurse, shall at length, be your Mother, and put you in Robes of Scarlet.

That is, by being a diligent apprentice, proudly wearing the "Prentices Cap," the boy would indeed prove to be the father of the man of honor. But not until Rousseau's day, when there was a blossoming romance between society and the family, when there was glory adorning the image of childhood, did the portraits of middle- and upper-class families capture in the clothing that they wore the segregation of children as a class.

89. *Helping Mother*, from *Children's Delight* (Boston, 1889). In assisting their mothers, young girls were preparing not only to relive their mothers' domestic lives, but were rising above their childhood toys as well.

Charity's children, the parish apprentices, were not merely working children, but were orphans or runaways or castoffs from families stricken by poverty, or from families that were unreclaimably irresponsible. Churchmen and town authorities had the power to take needy children from their parents and place them in private homes in their own parish counties. In a charitable spirit of community responsibility still in the medieval tradition, craftsmen were bound to the duty of accepting poor apprentices for work so that they might not turn to idleness, evil, and roguery. Masters were paid from local taxes to keep these children, and those who were wayward in their benevolent duties and refused the poor could, in turn, be taxed themselves by the town officials. The home and workshop served the parish apprentice in the same way that public institutions—poorhouse, hospital, orphanage, and detention center—would also serve society in later centuries. Unswervingly faithful to the apprenticeship system, most people believed that "as a twigge will best bend when it is greene, so children are fittest to be bound when they are young; otherwise by reason of their idle and base educations, they will hardly hold service." Interestingly, these words by one writer in the early 17th century echo the famous passage from Thomas Ingelend's book, *"The Disobedient Child* (c. 1560): "As long as the twig is gentle and pliant . . . with small force it may be bent."

The charity apprentice system, however, was not without its malefactors—masters who, after being paid the premium to board parish children, regularly returned to the parish for additional support. The guilds were equally guilty of maintaining an unfair control of the craft system by assigning the more lucrative crafts to the children of burgesses and owners of freeholds, while leaving poor children and orphans to the lesser trades. Regular beatings may have taken place in the houses of masters, but they were also common in the schools and in the houses of parents. Corporal punishment, after all, was then an accepted form of "teaching." One critical writer described the beating of a boy in 1699 as a "vile castigation," in which the boy's secret parts were used as an "anvil and were exposed to the immodest and filthy blows of the smiter." Nonetheless, until the middle of the 17th century, apprenticeships of any sort were still far better alternatives for children than being left to the street or without occupation at all. Even the worst-treated apprentice received some kind of training and education at a time when children left at home or on the streets were often little more than starvelings.

Records of the abuse of 18th-century apprentices appear in abundance in periodicals of the period. Midwives, tambourine makers, and cotton mill owners were among the masters often accused of ill-treating, underfeeding, and even murdering their charges.

The most common abuse was to send children out of their own counties far away from their parents and familiar neighborhoods for mere pragmatic reasons—one parish needing relief from the poor taxes, for example, or another parish needing additional apprentices for its factories. This practice was especially pronounced in England in the late 18th century until it was stopped in 1816 by a bill limiting the distance between the homes of parents and masters.

The evils of child labor in England and America were first made obvious in the cotton mills that frequently employed children as young as four years old. These children, in fact, made up as much as fifty percent of the work force at some mills. The Almy, Brown, and Slater Cotton Manufactory in Rhode Island, modeled on the English mills of Strutt and Arkwright, may be cited as typical of factory conditions in the late 18th and early 19th centuries. A child over seven worked from sunrise to sunset six days a week with two and a half days off a year; children between six and sixteen earned

90. *A Stitch in Time,* from *Children's Delight* (Boston, 1889). Little girls of the Victorian era devoted much of their play time to sewing reticules, bags, pincushions, and needlebooks for church bazaars. To labor over such trifles was called by the authorities of the day "amusing works"—a term that is explicit about the pleasure one was to derive from work.

slightly more than half a woman's wages and only a fourth of a man's. Similar conditions existed for children in the mines and in the domestic industries of silk and wool weaving, ribbon and stocking weaving, and glovemaking, where they worked in great number. But as bad as was the state of the working child in industry, he was even worse off in the homes and workshops of private families. Thousands of children were actually sold by their parents as slaves to chimney sweeps, mine owners, and other employers.

It is difficult to know the intricacies and the extent of the cruelties perpetrated on the working child before the Industrial Revolution, since very few working-class people left behind written records of their torment. The pages of such works as the *Tatler* and *Spectator* and Jonas Hanway's *Earnest Appeal for Mercy to the Children of the Poor* (1766), however, provide us with eye-opening hints as to how the law looked tolerantly upon those poeple who were treating children as spare parts for the gentry. As late as 1761 a beggar woman had received only two years in prison for putting out the eyes of her charges in order to derive a living from their "usefulness" as beggars. Children's teeth were also known to have been torn out and used afterwards as replacements in the mouths of the rich. Even in the parish workhouses, provided for children who were bastards or just too many in the household, what passed for "training" was little more than instruction in pickpocketing, shoplifting, and, for nine- and ten-year-old girls, trading as prostitutes. Given the horrors that faced the poor working child *before* the Industrial Revolution, one can understand why—20th-century antagonism to the machine notwithstanding—the coming of the machine production might have been viewed by the poor as a very welcome relief.

In response to the long-standing brutality and greed of men who deprived children of any semblance of humanity, such clergymen as John Cotton saw a ray of light for these mistreated children in encouraging men to find "a calling":

> If thou beest a man that lives without a calling, though thou has two thousand to spend, yet if thou hast no calling, tending to public good, thou art an uncleane beast.

The emphasis such churchmen placed on a calling—a particular occupation that would also help to fulfill God's plan—worked to control much insensitivity towards children, to counsel masters, and to teach apprentices that they had rights and that their labors were not only good but glorious. Each person was therefore advised of the "beauty" in labor.

Although many modern critics would be quick to point out the possible hypocrisy in the assumption that labor is beautiful, one cannot doubt that at the time this theological position was both sincere and comforting. Books, written specifically for apprentices by tradesmen, instructed working children that they, too, had a place in the kingdom if they cultivated the spirit and mind by reading their grammars and catechisms *while they were working at their labors.* (Years later, Thomas Hardy's Jude Frawley would do just that by studying his Latin grammar while driving his delivery wagon.) By the middle of the 17th century, then, young tradesmen had been successfully indoctrinated to be proud of their calling in society.

Apprenticeship for the poor did not work out well in America. Samuel Slater, the English-born manufacturer who employed poor and rural children in his Rhode Island mill, agreed with others that the American temperament was not suited to it and that it was simply not in the American spirit to apprentice anyone. Some modern critics, however, believe that a lack of public responsibility for the poor caused the failure of the apprenticeship system in America. Others see as a cause a colonial surplus of middle-class children, as well as of black, Indian, and white slaves and redemptioner's children still paying for their parents' voyages to America with their own indentured labor. As a result of the failure, however, vagrancy was a problem on the streets of early America.

In 1672 the colony of Virginia attempted to clear its streets of vagabond children by passing an act that empowered county courts to bind out the children of poor parents unable to place their offspring with tradesmen. Although other colonies passed similar acts, there were still few willing masters who would take on children of the poor. So callous was the treatment of the destitute, in fact, that some New Englanders devised an auction to sell off, singly or in groups, their poor—children and the aged alike. Public officials as early as 1646 placed boys and girls in flax houses, where from the ages of seven or eight they learned to card, knit, and spin in return for the bare necessities of life. What masters and public workhouses could not accomplish in dealing with the poor was left to benevolent societies, churches, women, trade unions, and factory owners. But their combined effort for Christian charity was at best scatter-shot since these charitable Americans were pitted against an inherited distrust of being landless, of having no material responsibility. Even for the republican Thomas Jefferson land was held to be concomitant with independence, and the working of it with being truly free.

By the late 18th century, at the beginning of the machine age, many Americans came to view child labor as a positive good. In 1767, for example, Sir Henry Moore, governor of New York, declared child labor a great moral service on the part of parents in the creation of a strong economy. He proclaimed enthusiastically that every house in his colony swarmed with working children. To Alexander Hamilton in the young republic, children carding, fulling, spinning, and helping in the production of homemade cloth were emblematic of national progress. Child labor, like *all* American labor, became, in effect, a patriotic act.

Economic independence from Britain came at a price, and American children helped to pay for it. The child was squeezed between a factory owner who gave him his wages and a father who took them from him. As in the English village of Bethnal Green—where little children were hired out to silk manufacturers for a pittance (2d. per week and tea) while parents received a pocketful (15s. 8d.)—Americans in the factory age wre no longer looking after children as masters had once looked after their apprentices. The poor working child was no longer a member of a family, no longer a student in the regular school, and no longer treated as an accepted member of the community. In short, he was for the first time in history not only a child, but a child separated from all other children.

91. *The Little Laborers of New York City,* artist unknown, American, c. 1890. The exploitation of children in American sweatshops rivaled that exposed by the pen of Charles Dickens in England in the 1840s. Before the photographs of such reformers as Lewis W. Hine—a "conscience with a camera"—stirred the nation, a few feeble outcries were to be found in such magazines as *Harper's.* These little girls toiled from 5:30 A.M. to 5:30 P.M. without a single break. If they dozed, they were kept awake by cold water dashed in their faces.

The factory system in the United States caused violent and opposing responses in the hearts of thoughtful men. Repetitive tasks, high regulation, and perfectionism were in-human and unchristian according to the predecessors of the Arts and Crafts movement of the late 19th century. And worst of all, according to such thinkers as the Reverend Horace Bushnell, the factory separated families as it destroyed the sanctity of the home.

On the other hand were the likes of Judge Joseph Story, who in 1819 saw the factory as a perfectionist's dream, a beautiful balance between commerce and agriculture, "between the learned professions and the mere proprietors of capital; between the day laborer and the unoccupied man of ease." One early 19th-century newspaper even compared the factory in America to an infant in its mother's arms. The mother's duty to care for her offspring was much like the government's responsibility for the manufactory and the mill owner's responsibility for working children. It was believed

92. *Factory Supervisor Beating Boy*, artist unknown, British, c. 1840. A third of England's textile workers were children. These "lively elves," as they were called, were preferred by many mill owners to adult laborers since they rarely complained and rarely became fatigued. Ironically, these children produced the cotton cloth that revolutionized the sanitary habits of the English, reducing the high rate of infant mortality for every class but their own.

that "cherishing" the factory, like "cherishing" the child, would repay the affectionate benefactor with peace and prosperity. In this spirit, such mill owners as the American Slater and the English Strutt and Arkwright provided rudimentary educations for the very young children in their manufactories. English readers, school bibles, Murray's Grammar, Walker's Dictionary, and the psalms and hymns of Isaac Watts were among the books that Slater bought for his child-laborers. Harriet Robinson, a young woman who worked in the mills at Lowell, Massachusetts, wrote glowingly of the experience:

> The discipline our work brought us was of great value. We were obliged to be in the mill at just such a minute, in every hour, in order to doff our full bobbins and replace them with empty ones. We went to our meals and returned at the same hour every day. We worked and played at regular intervals, and thus our hands became deft, our fingers nimble, our feet swift, and we were taught daily habits of regularity and of industry; it was, in fact, a sort of manual training or industrial school. Some of us were fond of reading, and we read all the books we could borrow. One of my mother's boarders, a farmer's daughter from the state of Maine, had come to Lowell to work for the express purpose of getting books, usually novels, to read, that she could not find in her nature place . . . . I had been to school quite constantly until I was nearly eleven years of age, and then, after going into the mill, I went to some of the evening schools that had been established, and which were always well filled with those who desired to improve their scant education, or to supplement what they had learned in the village school or academy.

93. *Child Labor,* artist unknown, American, 1888. Although several states passed laws limiting child labor to ten hours a day, extra work "with parental approval" was encouraged and was exempt from such "protection." Piecework in tenement houses, especially among immigrants, was endemic in American cities. These children, apparently the sole support of an invalided mother, work well into the early hours of morning stripping tobacco.

Americans were aware of the criticism aimed at European factories as seats of vice, immorality, sickness, and feudal degradation. But they believed that conditions were

94. *Newsboy*, G. F. Gilman, American, 1875. A school of late 19th-century painting (*see* figs. 83, 106, and plate XVIII) romanticized and effeminized working-class children, then referred to as "street urchins," so that in their cosmeticized states they bore little or no resemblance to the hard realities of the working child's life. Just how and why this type of painting rose to the great popularity it enjoyed has yet to be explained by art historians.

different in their own young country. They talked about what the machines could do for the poor Americans—how many they could clothe, and how equal and perfect society could become thereby. By a simple turn of the wheel and with little fingers on the bobbin, they could harmonize all the parts, as did God in his universe. Look at the factories at Lowell, one gentleman-farmer observed: "The moral spectacle here presented is in itself beautiful and sublime." The technology of the factory and the work of children signalled for many the triumph for all of mind over matter.

In the 19th century, laws and public institutions—orphanages, foundling homes, hospitals, asylums, schools—replaced parents, masters, and even factory owners as the guardians of poor apprentices and factory children. The first factory act in England (1802) legally separated orphaned apprentices from other workers and protected them simply because they were young. Children were protected against abuse from their own parents or from guardians. Eventually child labor laws were enacted on both sides of the Atlantic to protect youngsters from overwork and a life of illiteracy. Even the children of working-class parents who were not destitute received the legal right to an education. But these laws, which benefitted many children in the new republic, did not benefit all, slaves and Indian children, for example, faring even worse than poor whites.

The peculiar religious rationale for racial prejudice and for the intense mistrust of the poor, children included, was the same—God had planted these "unfortunates" among men as a challenge to Christian benevolence and to help believers overcome their own human deficiencies. The very real fear that educating the slaves and the poor would flood the work market and overthrow a society that was just being established was rarely verbalized, but was nonetheless intensely felt. Overwhelming and paralyzing were the unconscious fears of a people too frightened by the unknown to lend their neighbors a helping hand.

But abroad, at just the moment that Charles Dickens was undertaking the series of remarkable novels that were to etch indelibly on the public consciousness the plight of the wretched poor, his Victorian contemporary Elizabeth Barrett Browning had already written her lament to the working child:

> The young, young children, O my brothers,
> They are weeping bitterly;
> They are weeping in the playtime of the others
> In the country of the free.

95. *Two Boys with the American Flag*, artist unknown, 19th century.

6.

The Good Child and the Bad

Even a child is known by
his doings.
Proverbs 20:11

Today we use the phrase "the good child" as if we all knew exactly what it means, as if it were a concept treasured in the past as it is in modern times, and as if men have always cared whether a child were "good" or not. But "the good child" is a concept that did not concern the past as it seems to have plagued modern man, since there were no overriding rules or special standards for children that were not also applicable to the rest of medieval society. If by "good" we mean obedient, then everyone in medieval times was expected to be good. If by "good" we mean innocent, then no one in medieval times assumed goodness was possible on this earth. Consequently, children were not vehicles for innocence any more than they were vehicles for sin, and they most certainly were not the agents of salvation.

Medieval art identified a child by his toys or his nakedness or by his being partially clad in a shirt and cap, his bottom and his feet bare. Depicting a good child in medieval woodcuts, if being "good" simply referred to doing what was expected, meant picturing him at song with the choir rather than reading with the master, or holding quills and scrolls for transcribing music rather than reading from books. Like the rest of the community, good children were churchgoing, but not schoolgoing, and their lives were less complicated by ideas than by the stresses of a brutal physical environment. The child of the 15th century was considered good when he could work like an adult, understand his place in the world at large like an adult, fit into the manorial system like an adult, and direct all his loves and his labors to God like an adult. In other words, he was good when he had finally outgrown his childhood.

151

The frequency with which children in their natural and sensual condition were portrayed in 15th-century books of hours and church triptychs points up a remarkably casual approach on the part of medieval clergy and laity toward human functions which many moderns have condemned as "bad," sensual, or merely private. Children were depicted in crowded street scenes exposing themselves, urinating, being breast-fed or circumcised in public while groups of other children and adults mulled nearby looking on. These scenes were unself-consciously portrayed because children were not then judged as either innocent or corruptible. Their actions were part of the physical world common to every class and to every age group.

As we have already seen, masturbation in medieval children was not considered shameful. It did not bring with it the degradation or emotional strain of guilt which arose after the Reformation. One of the first treatises on the sexual behavior of children, written in the 15th century for church confessors, accepted a rather modern assumption, but one which frightened early reformers—masturbation, practiced by boys under twelve, was not only widespread, but inevitable. Although the author, Jean de Gerson, regarded early sexual activity as the result of original sin, medieval clergymen generally viewed such "pollution" as only one more item in an undiscriminating list of medieval sins which also included lying, cursing, swearing, sleeping late, and talking in church. At a time when even comtemplating suicide was a far greater sin than actual fornication or adultery, it is not surprising that classical literature which freely discussed "shameful acts" in vulgar speech were also treated lightly and were, in fact, read to children by their schoolmasters. By the end of the 16th century, when goodness was newly associated with innocence and innocence grew more valued than independence, the classics, like the minds of men, fell under the thrall of the censor.

An interest in good children—that is, in children who were obedient and innocent—blossomed with the moral reform of the 17th century. Protestant theologians began to lay heavier demands on children for perfection not only in themselves but for the whole race of men. Parents expected the child to be innocent of worldly knowledge and at the same time, strangely enough, to have the mature capacity to reason. They assumed that the child could grasp the abstraction of religious mystery, understand the nature of "the good life," and intuit what has always been almost incomprehensible to the mature mind—the overpowering experience of death. The good child in the 17th century was expected to know the pleasures of solitude, self-discipline, piety, literacy, and hard work, and to find and then sink with joy into the purifying experience of conversion.

Under the influence of this theological speculation, real children in the early modern period were reported to have been increasingly obedient and serious, compulsive and industrious. Trying to be "good," they faced a new and painful personal conflict—the loss of self-will, which among boys in particular had many repercussions. John Adams in the 18th century likened the task of Calvinistic goodness to Hercules choosing between the "Life of Effeminacy, Indolence and Obscurity, or a Life of Industry,

96. *The Good Girl and the Bad Boy,* artist unknown, American, c. 1870. If in society a male had every advantage over a female, a curious inversion occurred when in the 19th century womankind became enthroned. Young girls became described as "little angels," whereas their counterparts of the opposite sex were frequently called "little devils." Significantly, a 19th-century poet, Robert Southey, originated the rhyme that praised girls as consisting of "sugar and spice and all things nice," to the detriment of the "ingredients" of little boys: "snips and snails and puppy-dog tails."

Temperance, and Honour." Warning male students of the obstacles along the path to righteousness, he admonished them to 'Let no Girl, no Gun, no Cards, no flutes, no Violins, no Dress, no Tobacco, no Laziness, decoy you from your books." The dreadful conflict embodied in this understanding of "goodness," made very explicit by Philip Greven in *The Protestant Temperament*, was that while children were not to exhibit the weakness of women—the soft ways of luxury, extravagance, and ruin—yet they were not "good" unless they could also submit their wills, an act of surrender that was itself essentially "feminine." Boys were faced with temperamental, emotional, and sexual choices because the new vitality and glory of childhood made them separate, particular, and different from the independent, assertive, and now republican world of men.

As far back as the 17th century, books were generally considered good influences on children. Of the thousands of different books brought to New England before 1700, the first and largest category was religious and included sermons, catechisms, aids to piety, and concordances; the second was school texts; the third was bibles and psalm

97. *The Young Samuel Praying,* after Sir Joshua Reynolds, British or American, 19th century. Sir Joshua's original painting was among the most popularly reproduced works of art considered suitable for the walls of "good" youngsters (*see* plate XIX). The biblical Samuel was in every sense the perfect child because he was completely dedicated to the Lord.

books. What followed in popularity were romances and books on practical morality, essays, and philosophy. Modern English poetry, classical literature, geographies, dictionaries, biographies, and books on law, history, navigation, astronomy, cookery, and travel were shipped in much smaller numbers. Many of the same books were shared by adults and children alike. Although the pious, like the later evangelicals, did not approve of children reading romantic literature because it stirred the "common passions" without offering a moral point, the five invoices addressed in 1685 to John Usher, the leading book dealer in Boston, indicate that the fourth largest category of books imported to New England was romance and light fiction. The "how-to" books on worldly and spiritual advancement under God's jurisdiction were just behind the romances in popularity and offered advice on how to be a "good" merchant, how to be a "good" seaman, how to be a "good" husbandman, how to be a "good" gardener, and, of particular interest to us, how to be a "good" parent and how to be a "good" child.

Who were the "bad" children in the minds of early modern families? There must have been an abundance of them in America if the words of such clergymen as Jonathan Edwards that rang through New-World churches and schools are to be taken literally. Following in the ideological footsteps of his Puritan ancestors, he warned

98. *The Tease*, artist unknown, American, 19th century. Such pictures of childish mischief were common in the 19th century. Surprisingly, mischief—far from being considered evil—was considered by some acceptable as a natural trait of male children. Disobedience, which had been believed the primary *cause* of original sin in earlier centuries, became less offensive in the Victorian era then sensuality, the *result* of original sin. Consequently, mischief stemming from disobedience became a fitting subject for illustration and was even regarded as amusing or as "cute." The 20th-century reader, however, is quick to recognize that the little boy is actually "awakening" the girl's sensuality, but the Victorians would most rigorously have denied this.

18th-century parents to be suspicious of the appearance of innocence in children, since, without following God, such "innocence" was but a mask of the devil:

> As innocent as children seem to be to us . . . they are young vipers, and are infinitely more hateful than vipers, and are in a most miserable condition . . . . They are naturally very senseless and stupid . . . and need much to awaken them. Why should we conceal the truth from them?

The way for parents to fight evil in the child, therefore, was to confront him with it and to hope that he could quickly commit himself to God. Obviously, in the 17th century, as in the Middle Ages, ideas of good and bad were part of their own time, to be reckoned with today only by viewing them within the context of yesterday.

Childhood liberty, according to pious families, opened the doors to the evil of children in their natural, inherited, and rebellious state of sin. Disobedience, the original sin, was the first and most obvious offense to the "representatives of God," their parents. Even the merest look of discontent in performing childhood "duties" signalled an inward "rebellion" and an unwilling resignation, signs that the soul was breaking links in the universal chain of existence, and signs that the child did not believe in the sovereignty of God. Disobedience to the father and his authority and the consequent disruption of the family sense of order seemed to threaten the very structure of early modern society.

In addition to obviously rebellious behavior, bad children could be identified by other outward appearances or marks of the evil inner self. What they ate and what they wore, too, evidenced states of good or evil. Susanna Wesley, the mother of the founder of Methodism, raised her children in the belief that food, among other things, shaped and expressed a child's benevolent character and therefore had to be used as a tool to teach the restrictions of "goodness" as well as to nourish the child:

> Whatever they had, they were never permitted at those meals to eat of more than one thing, and of that sparingly enough. Drinking or eating between meals was never allowed, unless in case of sickness, which seldom happened. Nor were they suffered to go into the kitchen to ask anything of the servants when they were at meat: if it was known they do so, they were certainly beat, and the servants severely reprimanded.

Conversely, food was the great symbol of benevolence, even for the pious if, through the proper nourishment of a child's soul by his parents, he knew its eternal value and shared it—an idea illustrated in one of Maria Edgeworth's *Moral Tales* (1800):

> Since he had acquired other pleasures, those of affection and employment, his love of eating had diminished so much, that he had eaten only one of his radishes, because he felt more pleasure in distributing the rest to his mother and sisters.

Fine clothing was meant to cover up flaws in the character, according to pedagogical writers of the 18th century. John Wesley, in fact, interpreted fine style in clothes as signs of a defective education and a sure lack of piety. In females such finery could mean only the flaunting of their basic seductive passions. Plain clothes in reformed families, on the other hand, were outward signals of inner grace. Moreover, the association between clean clothes and goodness—a commonplace in the 18th and 19th centuries and by no means lost today—goes back at least to the 16th century when

99. *Be Kind to the Needy*, from *Picture Lessons, Illustrating Moral Truth* (Philadelphia, c. 1850). The original title of this illustration is explicit: "She is blind. The little girl leads her over the bridge very gently and puts her in the way to her humble home. A kind deed never goes unrewarded." Or as the Victorian maxim puts it: "Kindness is the sunshine in which virtue grows."

fines of a penny were levied for "wearing a foul shirt on Sunday."

Sloth, one of the "deadlier" sins, could be prevented in children, according to the popular American cleric John Barnard in *A Call to Parents and Children* (1737), by keeping them indoors "at their books and at some little service." Although Barnard was lenient in trying to divert children rather than beating them, his insistence that children be kept busy recalls the early Protestant association of idleness not only with the self-polluting sin of masturbation, but with something even worse—the "parasitic" life of the begging orders of the Catholic monasteries. Consequently, in their new doctrine of diligence and righteousness, the Protestant clergy believed that the poor got exactly what they deserved. Had not Saint Paul set the proper example when he said: "If any would not work, neither should he eat"? Within this context, Christian benevolence became impossible to define and diligence a difficult moral issue. As in their understanding of the state of childhood itself—one minute "full of warmth and heat"

100. *The Rogue Caught*, from *Picture Lessons, Illustrating Moral Truth* (Philadelphia, c. 1850). What boy, long grown up, cannot relive the anguish of a window broken in his youth? The pain of this boy's face travels easily across the centuries. But, as the original caption tells us, he has been bad—not because he broke the grocer's window, but because he failed to heed the grocer's warning of what might happen if he continued to play with his mischievous friends in front of the shop. Now, says the caption, having chosen not to hear, he must pay the consequences and replace the glass.

and in the next nothing but "indecencies and enormities"—Protestants were also ambivalent about what constituted the right state for benevolence.

Although sin had been generally accepted as the natural way of human life, it was not, however, irremediable in the eyes of humanists a century before the age of Puritanism. Vives, as early as 1524, wrote that idle parents were villainously to blame for idle children, and he suggested removing such children immediately to foundling homes, illustrating once again that there had been an immediacy about community problems before the Reformation and that the ruling authorities were then more than willing to remove children from the homes of abusive parents.

101. *"Sit Up, Ponto!"* artist unknown, American, 1868. Children were to train and discipline their pets for the understanding it gave them of their parents' treatment of themselves: "It may sometimes be necessary to use the whip *after* Ponto knows his duty," the original caption reads, "but never to teach with. Much kindness and patience will be needed, and for this reason it is well for children to train pets, for the good effects which it will be likely to have on themselves." The gentle benevolence advocated is pure 19th century; the analogy of children to animals is as old as time itself.

But although everyone in the decades that followed was aware of the dreadful conditions faced by the unwanted children of contemporary society—beggars, vagrants, child prostitutes, thieves—very few were willing to take responsibility for them. Under such desperate circumstances, government was not behaving insensitively when it disregarded the natural family and sent such children away at a young age to a community elsewhere for apprenticeship. The English were amazingly optimistic that a change in environment would bring about a change in the child, even though they realized, of course, that such benevolent actions served a practical function as well by reducing the

102. *The First Smoke*, artist unknown, American, 1870. In the last third of the 19th century, the mischievous boy became an accepted subject of popular literature and art. Mark Twain's Tom Sawyer, Huckleberry Finn, and Puddin'head Wilson were enormously successful characters as was Peck's Bad Boy, a lad who played endless practical jokes on his father. The century ended with the development of the comic strip, among whose first successful characters were the mischievous Katzenjammer Kids, The Yellow Kid, and Happy Hooligan. Although all of these characters contributed at least occasionally to "moral" conculsions, people obviously enjoyed them *because* they were mischievous. *The First Smoke* gives similar pleasure, its "message" notwithstanding.

tax burden. Young children were therefore moved not only to other parishes, but shipped to other countries in the belief that such separation would make honest boys out of beggars and perhaps saints out of thieves. In 1640 Anthony Abdy, a London alderman, left a bequest of money to be used expressly for "poore Boyes and Girles to be taken up out of the streets of London as Vagrants for the Cloathing and transporting of them to Virginia, New England or any other of the Western Plantations. . . ." His two sons also wrote similar wills.

The prevailing belief, hard as it might be for us to accept in the 20th century, was nonetheless clear: Apprenticeship, rewarded by active work and by money in a boy's pocket, prevented him from being deemed "bad" in the public eye. Conversely, poverty was considered the root cause of "badness." Or more specifically, the *idleness* of poverty was the sin that created the bad child. Despite occasional humanitarian complaints about child labor, an effort to put children to work who might otherwise be treated as bad or who, in fact, became bad was fairly consistent in the 18th and 19th centuries. By an act of 1703, English children were allowed to be put out to sea at the

103. *New England Interior*, Charles F. Bosworth, Sr., American, 1852. As a result of playing surreptitiously with a knife, the "bad" child has suffered the consequences. He is met, of course, by loving female attention. One imagines that chastisement followed first-aid.

age of ten, to serve until they reached the age of twenty-one and had learned to be useful in trade and navigation. Such clearing of the streets of "rogues" was regarded as patriotic and the Christian thing to do. With the help of a new marine association and a group of merchants, bankers, and shipowners, St. John Fielding, an English magistrate

104. *The Red Cross,* artist unknown, American, c. 1890. The ready acceptance of the mischievous child as a literary and artistic motif was sufficiently widespread for it to have appeared in commercial advertisements with humorous appeal. The Red Cross Base Burner apparently generated a great deal of heat!

inspired by the act of 1703, developed a society to fit out and send to sea more than 10,000 boys. Fielding also proposed a "preservatory" or "reformatory" to serve girls already prostitutes who were willing to be reformed. Incorporating both the benevolent and practical sides of contemporary Christianity, this institution would train wayward girls in domestic science and also double as a public laundry. Upon graduation, the girls could be placed as servants in respectable households provided that they learned well and that good masters and mistresses could be found as guardians. Trained to spin, to knit stockings, to make artificial flowers, toys, gloves, and carpets, they could sell their wares and thereby contribute to their own upkeep. Fielding's proposal eventually found expression in the "Female Orphan Asylums" that soon followed.

The public facilities for "problem" children in America were even more limited than

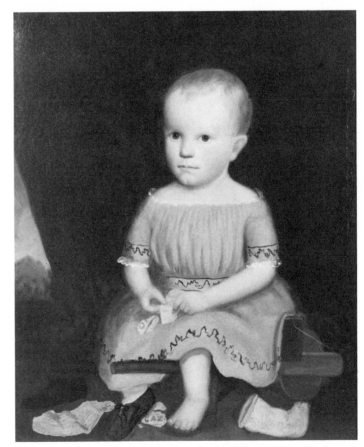

105. *The Torn Gazette,* artist unknown, American, 19th century. Human innocence is not without its element of mischievousness, a fact recognized as long ago as the 17th century when George Herbert wrote: "Better a snotty child than his nose wiped off." This little boy has been busily tearing up a newspaper and, like children in every era, has happily removed one shoe and sock. As in the nursery rhyme, "one shoe off and one shoe on" suggests the little devil submerged within the child and is a motif frequently found in painting (*see* plate XX).

in the mother country. Except for the orphanage founded in 1739 by the evangelists John Joachim Zubly and George Whitefield, colonial children were put into alms-houses, mixing freely with the diseased and the insane until they were old enough to be bound out in service. With the exception of these pestilent almshouses, there were no other facilities for such children in America during the 18th century.

By the 19th century, the "bad" child—idle, illiterate, poor, obscene, or just plain mischievous—was easy to spot in the street and in the home. The "good" child, however, was less easy to identify, describe, or raise to maturity. Aware of the evils of drink, ostentation, dance and other forms of immoderate behavior, evangelical children were taught the struggle, the doubt, and the frailty of goodness. For them it was an impossible aim, and endless battle. The children of genteel and moderately religious families, however, were relatively untroubled with the outward signs of "goodness" and were comfortable whether they were at play or at prayer, whether they learned the

106. *The First Cigarette,* D. Wilson, American, late 19th century. Surrounded by the disorder of poverty and lighting up a smoke that hardly seems his first, this fellow has one shoe off and a hole in his sock as well. But the whole scene, including his threads and patches, is so artificially contrived as to render suspect the late 19th-century fascination with "street urchins." The modern reader has the uneasy feeling of viewing an 18-year-old adolescent transmogrified somehow into a cute 10-year-old.

music of the guitar or whether they studied the classics or theology. But for all children in the 19th century, goodness had become at least a matter of progress and achievement—boys were to prepare for an honorable place in public life and girls were to master the management of the home. Not unlike the medieval hierarchy of the sexes, achievement according to sex was part of being good. If 19th-century life could be likened to the articulated cogs and wheels of a machine, then each sex had its prescribed parts within that machine: the young girl was ordained to perfect the "machine of the family," and the boy was to perfect the machine of the factory.

Among those who worked to perfect the machinery of the family, the Reverend Horace Bushnell and the writer Catherine Beecher were perhaps the foremost. Although Bushnell understood that not every child would be "perfected" simply because he had been brought up in a good home (just as not every child would emerge a scholar who went to school), he urged parents nonetheless to perfect their homes, to make them "sacred," and, insofar as possible, to make the home as "good" as the church. "The table and hearth," in other words, were to become (in Bushnell's phrase) "a holy rite and life itself an element of saving power." Although for some Bushnell was secularizing what had always been spiritual, for others he was allowing the benevolence of Christianity to be applied in a practical way. Parents were to teach by example and were to aim for voluntary submission as the child learned to understand what was "good." Consequently, Bushnell observed that children's willfulness or mischief was not "so purely bad or evil as it seemed." Original sin, he emphasized, was what parents in their *own* imperfectness transmitted to children after the moment of birth, and largely through poor upbringing and teaching.

Since in the age of the machine the man of the family had long left home for work and no longer offered his children or his servants the educational or religious training that once was his responsibility alone, women accepted the task of teaching everyone in the household. Even if they never married, never had a natural family, they were encouraged by such writers as Catherine Beecher to be "mothers of the needy." In her books on the American home and on the training of young girls, Miss Beecher was both loving and restrictive with the young "moulders of the Republic," as she called American womanhood. She applauded domestic manual labor, and, like the theologians and physicians of earlier centuries, she tried to convince girls of the beauty in nursing the newborn, a privilege that belonged by nature to the female sex alone. She blamed religion and education for "conspiring to degrade the family State," and, though she herself was a maiden lady, she sanctified the mothering experience, whether it was of natural children or of orphans, or of "the sick, the homeless, or the sinful." This most ardent of Victorian women epitomized what most of the little children's books, Sunday-school texts, and ladies' magazines of the period were trying to teach mothers and children in their florid and occasionally bizarre moral pages—that the act of *doing* good was the act of *being* good; that good works punctuated faith; that benevolence was what the religious revival was all about; and that a self-sacrificing womanly instinct would reign in the new nation to bring about a state of universal goodness.

Catherine Beecher, echoing the new confidence of 19th-century females in their "instinctual" urge to nurture, raised the virtues of motherhood to a state that had not been seen since the veneration of the Holy Mother centuries before. Protestants and the new republican nation may have eschewed all icons that smacked of "popery," but ap-

107. *Black and White*, artist unknown, American, 19th century. Although the original intention of this painting is vague—the Negro was as badly treated in art as he was in real life—there is no question whatever as to which of the two children is the bad child and which the good. The symbolism is perhaps unintentional, but one can hardly imagine a more succinct summation of a sad chapter in the history of the children of man.

parently many still yearned for the spiritual beauty of the Holy Family and for a sense of Christian community. Beecher's family plan, which she included in *The American Family Home*, outlined an ideal neighborhood in which homes revolved around a small church and a schoolhouse run by benevolent and intelligent women who were "pining for an opportunity to aid in carrying the Gospel to the destitute . . . [and] in training our whole race for heaven."

At the moment that Miss Beecher was envisioning the enthronement of the Christian woman, the growth of 19th-century cities was creating new problems for those who were "pining for an opportunity" to prove the perfectability of the human heart. Such contemporary men of letters as the American Ralph Waldo Emerson and Henry David Thoreau and the English novelist Charles Dickens had so capitalized on the evils of the city, as had Blake and Wordsworth in the previous generation, that it was virtually impossible to picture a good child surviving in the squalor of the streets. Obviously, the cities were breeding places of moral crapulence: little children smoked, drank, gambled and shared all the other sins that men have always passed on easily to boys and girls roaming idly in the city. With the ugliness exposed to the "bad" child growing more and more real, the "good" country child—in literature and in art, at least—became larger than life. Capturing the ideal of "goodness" and "folksiness," he seemed lost in the past, a veritable symbol of hope and innocence in his simple clothing—clothing that was soon aped by the fashionable in the city. Mid-19th-century portraits of children from the middle and upper classes show these urban children in the clothing—in the overalls and caps—of the farmer. The uniform of the agrarian worker was all that was left of what was meant by a "good" day's work.

An American spiritual revival in 1858, a burst of energy to do good which derived not from the clergy, the "country folk," or from women but from the cities, the factories, and from businessmen, was called by some people a miracle. "A hunger for cohesion" is how the historian Perry Miller described the phenomenon of union meetings within the factories where all sects and ages sang hymns together. Could it be that by including poor city children who needed a place in which to learn skills and who needed to be off the streets, the factory system represented a revival of "community" that had been lost since the Middle Ages? Only a few intellectuals criticized this brief spiritual revival as no better than a mechanics' fair or a cattle show, but business and religion had united in the city, however briefly, and the hope remained that their union would benefit the poor.

Not everyone approved of the perfectionism of the evangelicals, of the requirements of technology, of a growing nationalism on both sides of the Atlantic that saw in its mills and factories the symbols of national strength and political power. Not everyone was overjoyed to see the brilliant mechanical mind of the 19th century inventing machines that could dig, propel, pump, hammer, card, spin, weave, wash, cook, and print. Such humanitarians and men dedicated to the crafts as John Ruskin and William Morris resented the machine for its perfectionism and for the slavery that such perfectionism imposes. Man and his products were not intended to be perfect, they said. Nevertheless, the invention of the machine and the respect for what it could do for society raised the level of common labor, both of man and of his child.

As a consequence, Victorian children struggled under the combined burden of being perfect for their families, of being proficient workers, and of making perfect products in the factories. In short, they were well on the way to becoming standardized children,

108. *Girl by the Seashore*, artist unknown, American, 19th century. Like a 19th-century Venus emerging from the sea, this girl, on the verge of young womanhood, evokes an essential Victorian theme: the awakening of sensuality (*see* fig. 98 and plate XIX). If Wordsworth recognized in the seashell a "mysterious union with the native sea," many other poets likened the sea itself to the Eternal Woman, or as Emerson put it, the "nourisher," or as Donne, the "purifier." "The Sea," Edwin Markham wrote, "is Woman." Contained within this quintessentially good child of the 19th century is what the 17th century had known all along: the young are indeed the children of Adam and Eve.

mass-produced like most everything else in the 19th century. Only ministers and mothers were left to pick up the human pieces that they themselves had helped to break in the struggle.

But in the midst of the tension, in the shadow of the new technology and science, the understanding light of Sigmund Freud provided a new perspective for the family and the child. Not accepting the pious assumption of goodness, or the ability of man to understand all there was to know in himself, Freud returned, like the Romantics at the beginning of the century, to the innocence of childhood as an answer to "the good life." Freud believed that the initial human relationship between mother and child—as precious and as sacred as that of the first mother and child—held the primary source of all hope in life. Trust was built in that "intimate meeting of partners," providing the basis for a life of love and work and hope for the future. On such hope he laid the other virtues of traditional religion—purpose, love, care, and commitment—growing with the active "initiating" life and forming an independent and trusting soul. To understand the child, in whom resides the eternal source of all goodness and spirituality, was, for Freud, to understand the man.

Acknowledgements

The history of childhood is, remarkably, a relatively new subject of inquiry. (*The History of Childhood Quarterly*, for example, was founded as recently as 1973.) My greatest debt in preparing this book, therefore, is to the authors whose research has given us the pioneering knowledge we now have of this intriguing subject. In particular, I am grateful to the following scholars, whose works—listed in the bibliography—have been of inestimable value: Phillipe Aries, Robert H. Bremner, Lloyd deMause, Emory Elliott, J. William Frost, Philip Greven, Christopher Hill, Joseph F. Kett, Peter Laslett, Perry Miller, James Obelkevich, Ivy Pinchbeck and Margaret Hewitt, J. H. Plumb, and especially Lawrence Stone.

Many of the illustrations in this book could not have been reproduced without the generous co-operation of Clifford Schaefer, curator for the collection of Colonel and Mrs. Edgar William Garbisch; Israel Sack, Inc.; William Stahl and Nancy Druckman of Sotheby Parke Bernet, Inc.; Martha Fleischman of Kennedy Galleries, Inc.; Bernard and S. Dean Levy; and H. & R. Sandor. In addition, I acknowledge the assistance of Cheryl Wacher, Metropolitan Museum of Art; Anita Duquette, Whitney Museum of American Art; Ross Urquhart, Massachusetts Historical Society; Roberta Deveno, Museum of Fine Arts, Springfield, Massachusetts; David Deitch, Museum of Fine Arts, Boston; Lynn E. Springer and Louis Walker, St. Louis Art Museum; James Ayres, The John Judkyn Memorial; Beatrice Taylor and Catherine McKenny, The Henry Francis du Pont Wintherthur Museum; Dorothy Schling, Scott-Fanton Museum; Ira Bartfield, National Gallery of Art, Smithsonian Institution; Lilian Randall, Walters Art Gallery; and Joyce Guiliani, Yale Center for British Art.

Finally, for assistance with research and in the preparation of the manuscript, I would very much like to thank D. W. Robertson, Jr., Emory Elliott, Orrin Wickersham June, Bonnie Dawson, Andrea Graham, Nicholas Schorsch, Doris Dinger, and Martin Greif, editorial director of The Main Street Press.

Credits

Albany Institute of History and Art, 31; Bettman Archives, Inc., 49, 60, 61, 86, 91, 92, 93; British Museum Library, 5, 10, 69; City Art Museum, Manchester, 16; Colonial Williamsburg, 30; Fruitlands Museum, IX; Collection of Edgar William and Bernice Chrysler Garbisch, X, XVI, XX; Greenfield Village and Henry Ford Museum, IV; Guildhall Library, Aldermanbury, London, 11, 46.

The John Judkyn Memorial, 38, 77; Kennedy Galleries, Inc., 23, 57; Bernard & S. Dean Levy, Inc., 17, 65, 66, 80; Louisiana State Museum, 15; Massachusetts Historical Society 63, 87, 103 (gift of Sibylla Young), XV; Memorial Hall Museum, 35; Metropolitan Museum of Art, 18, 24 (gift of Edgar William and Bernice Chrysler Garbisch), 27, 47, I, VI (gift of Edgar William and Bernice Chrysler Garbisch), XI, XIV (gift of Edgar William and Bernice Chrysler Garbisch); Museum of Fine Arts, Boston, 39 (M. and M. Karolik Collection), II (ibid); Museum of Fine Arts, Springfield, 7, 8, XVIII.

Museum of the City of New York, 40, 54, 58 (The J. Clarence Davies Collection), 94; National Gallery of Art, Washington, D.C., 4, V (gift of Edgar William and Bernice Chrysler Garbisch), XII (ibid); National Gallery of Canada, 3; New York State Historical Association, Cooperstown, 9, 34, 37, VII, XIII; Philadelphia Museum of Art, 2, 14, XIX; Private Collections, 12, 56, 72, 96, 101, 102; Abby Aldrich Rockefeller Folk Art Center, Williamsburg, Virginia, VIII; Israel Sack, Inc., 21, 71, 98, 105; St. Louis Art Museum, 52, 73, 81.

H. & R. Sandor, Inc., 43; Shelburne Museum, 79; Sotheby Parke Bernet, Inc., 1, 6, 20, 22, 25, 26, 28, 32, 33, 36, 44, 53, 55, 70, 74, 75, 76, 78, 83, 95, 97, 106, 107, 108; Smith College Museum of Art, 67; Stanford University Museum of Art, 62 (Stanford Family Collection); Vassar College Art Gallery, 64; Whitney Museum of American Art, III, IV (gift of Edgar William and Bernice Chrysler Garbisch); collection of Printed Books and Periodicals, Winterthur Library, Winterthur, Delaware, 13, 19, 41, 42, 45, 48, 50, 51, 59, 68, 84, 85, 88, 89, 90, 99, 100, 104; Yale Center for British Art, 29 (Paul Mellon Collection); Yale University Art Gallery, 82 (The Mabel Brady Garvan Collection).

Bibliography

Aries, Phillipe. *Centuries of Childhood.* Translated by Robert Baldick. New York: Vintage Books, 1962.

Bremner, Robert H., ed. *Children and Youth in America,* Vol. I. Cambridge, Mass.: Harvard University Press, 1970.

deMause, Lloyd, ed. *The History of Childhood.* New York: The Psychohistory Press, 1974.

Demos, John. *A Little Commonwealth.* London: Oxford University Press, 1970.

Elliott, Emory. *Power and the Pulpit in Puritan New England.* Princeton, N.J.: Princeton University Press, 1975.

Erikson, Erik H. *Insight and Responsibility.* New York: W. W. Norton & Company, Inc. 1964.

Frost, J. William. *The Quaker Family in Colonial America.* New York: St. Martin's Press, 1973.

Greven, Philip. *The Protestant Temperament.* New York: Alfred A. Knopf, 1977.

Hill, Christopher. *Society and Puritanism in Pre-Revolutionary England.* London: Secker & Warburg, 1964.

Kett, Joseph F. "The American Family as an Intellectual Institution 1780-1880," paper presented at Davis Center Seminar, Princeton University, 21 April 1978.

_____ . "Adolescence and Youth in Nineteenth-Century America." In *The Family in History: Interdisciplinary Essays.* Ed. Theodore K. Rabb, and Robert I. Rotberg. New York: Harper & Row, 1971. pp. 95-110.

Laslett, Peter. *The World We Have Lost.* New York: Charles Scribner's Sons, 1973.

Levy, Barry John. "Tender Plants: Quaker Farmers and Children in the Delaware Valley, 1681-1735," paper presented at the Davis Center Seminar, Princeton University, 17 February 1978.

Miller, Perry. *The Life of the Mind in America.* New York: Harcourt, Brace & World, Inc., 1965.

_____ . *The New England Mind: From Colony to Province.* Boston: Beacon Press, 1961.

Kiefer, Monica. *American Children Through Their Books 1700-1835.* Philadelphia: University of Pennsylvania, 1948.

Obelkevich, James. *Religion and Rural Society.* Oxford: Clarendon Press, 1976.

Opie, Iona and Peter. *Children's Games in Street and Playground.* Oxford: Clarendon Press, 1969.

Pinchbeck, Ivy and Hewitt, Margaret. *Children in English Society Volume I.* Toronto: University of Toronto Press, 1969.

Plumb, J. H. "The New World of Children in Eighteenth-Century England." In *Past & Present* 67 (May 1975): 64-95.

Stone, Lawrence. *The Crisis of the Aristocracy 1558-1641.* London: Oxford University Press, 1977.

_____ . *The Family, Sex and Marriage in England 1500-1800.* New York: Harper & Row, 1977.

_____ . "Literacy and Education in England 1640-1900." In *Past & Present* 42 (February 1969): 69-139.

Thompson, Craig R. *Schools in Tudor England.* New York: Cornell University Press, 1958.

Watson, Foster. *The Beginnings of the Teaching of Modern Subjects in England.* London: Sir Isaac Pitman & Sons, Ltd., 1909.

Wright, Louis B. *Middle-Class Culture in Elizabethan England.* Chapel Hill: The University of North Carolina Press, 1935.

Index